Remember to Breathe

Growing Through the Stages of Grief

Remember to Breathe

Growing Through the Stages of Grief

By Evelyn Fannell

Remember to Breathe

Contents

Dedication:

For my husband, Jeff. Thank you for always being there for me, ready to step in and fix whatever might be broken, even when it is not humanly possible to do so. So very thankful that whenever I look up, you are there.

For my girls, Brandi and Jasmine. I know things are extra hard on you. I call to check on you more and expect you to answer more than I have in this "after" than I did in our "before," if that's even possible. But I thank you for being patient with me and allowing me to crowd your space and for understanding my need to do so, even when you'd rather not.

For my grandson, Christian. You remind me more and more of your Uncle Joe. Thank you for not running away from that. Thank you for reminding me that I'm pretty, especially for a grandma and for being so brutally honest in telling me when I'm not, but in a funny way. Something else Joseph did so often and that I miss so much. And thank you for being my buddy, calling me just because.

All of you give me the courage, the strength and the conviction to get out of bed every morning. You have and you continue to be my inspiration. I love you all more with each passing day.

And for my Joseph. My heart broke in pieces that day I lost you, and although the pieces continue to break sometimes, they are slowly being put back together because I know that one day, I will see you again. I love you with every part of my being and miss you just as much. Still. And always.

Acknowledgments

When we lost Joseph, I had no inclination on writing about it, much less talking about it, although I've been writing for most of my adult life. When God put that pen in my hand almost the day after and told me to write, little did I know I was writing the book. Two months later, nine chapters of the book were written. And I am so grateful to God for allowing me to write. In doing so it has helped me to grieve. And I am grateful for those who continued to cheer me on in the process, even when I felt like giving up.

To Pastor Hackett: Although we often look for confirmation, God doesn't need it, He just needs our obedience. So, I thank you for your obedience in preaching the word that day. I don't remember the title of the message, but three times you said, "Write the Book." And so it is written.

To Patricia: For checking in on me every single week since Joseph died and never missing a Thursday.

To my mom, Teddi Brockett: For the daily 9 a.m. phone calls. It's unfortunate to have to share grief and the loss of a child with anyone, let alone your mom, but I am grateful to have you, always encouraging me to write and to share while understanding how hard it is to do so.

To the family and friends who filled in the gap: I couldn't begin to name you all. But please know that your phone calls and texts often came at just the right time and have not gone unnoticed.

To my therapist, Dr. Danielle Jean-Pierre: You were so warm and opening from the first day we met, always encouraging me that there was more to me than I ever thought there was. You gave me confidence and strength even before I knew I needed to have it. Thank you for allowing God to use you.

To Michael Ashley: For your insight and creativity in editing and publishing my book. I truly appreciate your value, input, and expertise.

To my God: I of all people often felt like, and still do feel like, doubting Thomas. But Thomas knew one thing when Jesus revealed Himself to him: who God was. And the more things I continue to grow through, the more Jesus reveals Himself to me and I suppose, like Thomas, that's all I need to know as well.

Who Jesus is. He is my Lord and my God. Through it all. And for that I am thankful.

For more information about Joseph, please visit www.josephmfannellmemorialfund.org or Facebook @ripjoefannell.

Prologue

"This is officer Smith. I'm calling to let you know your son has been in an accident ..."

An accident? I felt like I couldn't breathe.

"He's been taken to Capital Health Hospital," the man on the line continued. More sounds came from the phone, but the words wouldn't connect in my mind. There had to be some mistake. "Joseph?"

"Yes. He was hit by another driver. They airlifted him—paramedics are helping him now. We don't have much information other than that he's in critical condition."

Nothing seemed real after that. Not hanging up. Not calling Jeff.

"Joseph was in an accident," I told him, as I tried to control the tears streaming down my face.

Not Jasmine making an airline reservation to get me back to New Jersey, either. I was in Chicago visiting her and as soon as the call ended, we huddled in her bedroom, embracing as if we could squeeze our fears from each other.

My phone rang again. It was Jeff calling back. "I just left the meeting. You know what hospital they took Joseph?"

Just a few months ago, my son began working for his father and Jeff had been expecting him in by 10 that morning. When Joe had not arrived, Jeff had called me earlier to find out where he was. I would later learn Joe's accident was at 9:57. He was just three minutes shy of arriving.

Jasmine looked on as my husband and I talked, wondering if her brother would be okay. *Would he?* The more I told Jeff what little I knew the more my heart sank. I couldn't talk long before I had to call the hospital back. I left a message for the on-duty ER surgeon, then began dialing number after number, sharing news about Joseph and asking friends to pray.

At last, the on-duty ER surgeon at Capital returned my call.

"Joseph has suffered a severe brain injury," he said.

Once again, I felt like I couldn't breathe. The walls were closing in—suffocating me.

"There is only one option," he continued. "We can try to repair the damage by draining fluid, but it's risky."

"Risky?"

"There's a good chance it will leave Joseph in a vegetative state."

"You mean temporarily?" I held onto a chair to steady myself.

"No. I'm afraid not. It could be permanent. But we need to make a choice now. There's no time to delay. Our window of operating is closing fast."

There is a reason we gasp for air. Once the body lets in breath, this allows us to go on. My whole world had come apart—my 22-year-old son might never walk, never talk, never do anything ever again. And yet here I was, remembering to breathe. To receive life.

"Mrs. Fannell?"

"Yes, I am here."

"What do you choose to do?"

But this wasn't a choice at all. "There has to be another answer."

"There isn't, Mrs. Fannell."

"Well, I can't choose that. I won't. I have to talk to my husband."

"Okay, do that, please. And then get here as soon as you can."

We ended the call. This time, I called Brandi, my older daughter in New Jersey.

"Joseph was in a car accident. I don't know much. But he's not doing well. Can you get to him so he won't be alone?

"What happened, Mom?"

"I ... don't know. Just please go to the hospital as soon as you can."

Thick afternoon traffic had backed up on the highway as was the norm in Chicago, no matter the time of the day, giving me time to call more friends and relatives as I made my way to O'Hare Airport.

The trip back East takes five hours, door to door, but I lost all sense of time in transit. During the flight I watched business travelers and families on their way home. Typing on laptops. Hugging. Chatting on phones. Reading magazines. Being normal. I longed for their peace of mind, their carefree smiles. *To go back to before.*

But as I flew through the midwestern skies, I began to wake up to a new truth: You can never go back. What must have been an ordinary night to everyone around me was the darkest moment of my life.

Chapter 1: Shock

Shock: A sudden upsetting or surprising event or experience.

Fluorescent light from the emergency room hallway shone into Jeff's face. He appeared so sad it was hard to look at him knowing my own pain was reflecting in his eyes. Until then I had managed to console Jasmine before I left, hugged a friend who greeted me at the airport, and somehow kept it together. But when my husband took me in his arms, I nearly collapsed.

Usually, Joseph is a heavy breather, but I had to listen for his breath, for a heartbeat. I needed to hear him. Hospital noises surrounded us—beeps and monitors going off, the chatter of personnel rushing about, but together we were quiet. I thought that if only we stayed still maybe Joseph would be okay.

Even before this, Jeff and I were survivors. We had made it through so much as a family. Early in our marriage, before we had Joseph, when we were building a life for ourselves in New York, the struggles began, often involving hospitals like this. During the second week of August 1988, I went to a doctor's appointment. I was eight months pregnant, so this was to be one of my last visits before giving birth. It was an exciting time for us. We already had Brandi, who was 6½. We had not yet learned our new baby's sex, choosing instead to be surprised when our new child came.

But this visit wasn't like all the others. The others were "well-visits," as our OBGYN called them. Upon examination that day, the doctor informed us our baby had stopped growing in my womb and they needed to schedule a C-section. So, on August 30, two weeks short of my due date, our daughter Jasmine came into the world weighing only 4 pounds. We looked forward to holding her, but she couldn't breathe. The doctors had to perform drastic procedures just to save her life. They plugged her into an oxygen machine to breathe for her. Two days later, the hospital discharged me, but they kept my baby girl.

A day later we returned. This time I wore a special hospital gown and gloves so as not to spread germs to our daughter and the other babies in the neonatal care unit. While there, I was struck by a piercing cry from another mom. A young mom had just learned that her baby died. My heart ached for her. There is no pain worse than losing a child as a parent, I thought—even back then.

But Jeff and I were fortunate that summer. We didn't lose our baby. Though suffering from asthma and jaundice, and despite the fact her lungs hadn't fully developed, Jasmine clung on. My girl was a fighter. Little could I ever dream back then that my baby girl would one day resemble the 22-year-old boy before me—you see, both were covered in wires. The first time I saw Jasmine they had shaved her head so they could place an IV in her. From the incubator where they placed her, I could see thin wires stemming from the small tubes taped to her tiny belly.

Now as Jeff led me inside Joseph's hospital room, I had to gasp.

Shock has a way of blocking out all kinds of emotion, all kinds of feelings. It sort of takes you into another realm, out of your body, out of the circumstance, someplace else. It freezes time.

"Watch out for his wires," a nurse warned me as I went to touch him.

Hand to my mouth, I held my breath as I took in all of the machines and tubes surrounding my son. Joseph had always been such an energetic kid, the kind who liked to shoot hoops for hours. Now he looked so frail and damaged only wires could hold him together.

"Oh Joseph," I cried out.

"Please, Mrs. Fannell," the nurse said. "Don't get too close. One of the wires might slip."

Moving slowly, delicately, I reached for his hand, kissing his forehead.

"Joseph, it's your mother. I know you can hear me. I'm back from Chicago. You can wake up now. Don't be afraid. You're gonna be all right. We're all here with you."

I saw his eyelids jump.

"You can hear me." I said, trying to be stern. "That's enough now, Joe, open your eyes."

Jeff stood by me. Together we prayed for our son.

"His eyelids moved, how could that be?" I asked the nurse. "I saw a raised eyebrow, too."

"It's involuntary," said the doctor from behind me.

It was the same one who had pressured me about the risky procedure while I was back in Chicago. I didn't like his tone and tried to ignore him, focusing instead on Joseph's face, praying he would wake up.

The more I looked at Joseph, the more memories came rushing back. *Other hospital visits.* Joseph as a baby—Joseph, who was also born with complications but fought back. Things were tough for him, too, in those early days. We didn't even have health insurance. Knowing he would have to be born at a city hospital, we came up with a plan: I would feign labor pains to go to a nice private hospital. Sure enough, Jeff drove me to the hospital of our choice, 10 days before my due date and told the triage nurse I was in labor.

As it turned out, I labored for the next 36 hours, determined to have a natural childbirth. But all that straining took a toll on Joseph. He went into distress, prompting my third and final C-section. Born with an imperforate anus, Joseph had to have a colostomy the morning after his birth to survive. Two other surgeries followed to correct his condition.

The first year presented more challenges for us, like learning how to take care of him and preparing for so many surgeries. We still had two young daughters at home and would take turns sleeping with Joseph while he was in the hospital. Meanwhile, Jeff attended law school. We had just the one car, yet somehow my husband managed to go back and forth, picking up our daughters from day care or school, dropping them off each morning, then returning to class, trying to study all the while our son was in the hospital.

Little Joseph also suffered from bronchitis. Like Jasmine, he often had to take nebulizer treatments to breathe freely. We spent more time in the hospital with Jasmine and Joseph back then than some people see in a lifetime. So much sickness—so much suffering—and all this before the boy was 5 years old.

Ignoring the doctor behind me, I continued praying over my Joseph, looking deep into my son's face, forcing myself to breathe—breathe through the pain and the fear. I felt Jeff's arm on my back, offering me strength. My eyes happened to land on a speck of dried blood on Joseph's cheek and suddenly he became that 5-year-old boy in my mind again.

By the age of 5, Joseph had beaten all the odds. A true survivor in the fashion of my family, he had come back from all of his illnesses, all of the problems we thought would prevent from living a normal life. He had grown healthier, stronger. He was also beautiful on the inside and out, a tall and thin muscular boy who liked to play with others but at the same time had no problem showing true affection, especially to me.

"Mommy! Mommy!" I heard him shouting from outside the house one day.

Jeff was carrying him when they entered, and as I saw the blood, I nearly fainted.

"What happened to your face?" I asked.

"He fell off his bike," Jeff explained.

Joseph had a small cut on his forehead, but he was covered in blood. It was not nearly as bad as all the blood made it seem, but still, I saw his life pass before my eyes. How I wished things could be so simple again—how I wished Joseph was only suffering from a minor bike accident right now.

"Mr. and Mrs. Fannell," the doctor said, interrupting my thoughts. "Now that you are both here, I wish to discuss the procedure I mentioned on the phone."

"What kind of operation is this?" Jeff asked.

"We need to drill a hole into your son's skull to drain the excess fluid."

"But didn't you say that could leave him … in a vegetative state?" Jeff could hardly get the words out.

"There is a high probability doing so could lead to Joseph being on life support indefinitely."

Jeff went quiet. So did I.

"You need to make a decision. Without this operation, your son will not survive."

"I cannot do that to Joseph," I told Jeff before stepping outside. I needed to go. I couldn't bear to talk to this doctor anymore. There was no hope in the man. Nothing he said inspired me to believe he could actually help my son. I worried about leaving Joseph for even a moment, but it was important to not say anything that might make the situation worse.

As I returned to the hallway, a feeling came over me that I hesitate to call dread. Like anyone, I had known fear, but never like this. Shock is a better word. Deep down I knew from the moment I saw Joseph that he was going to die, but this wasn't supposed to be. His last words to me had been, "I love you Mom."

His eyes were wide open then.

During the time we were in Joseph's room the waiting room had filled with friends and family: my sister and brother-in-law, people from our church, and Brandi. She had returned to the hospital after picking up her son, Christian. In spite of my dread, seeing them boosted my hopes. Gathered together, we tried to keep up our spirits; a hand on a knee here, an arm around a shoulder there, but we never took our gaze off what was happening with Joseph beyond the steel hospital doors just down the hall.

We all wanted to believe Joseph would make it through—this bright star of a young man—this sensitive, deep individual who could captivate a room of strangers with his poetry. The kind of young man who could bring you to tears by revealing the vastness of his imagination through spoken word and rhymes that sounded as if they came from someone decades older. It was poetry in motion when he performed and sometimes it made me squirm in my seat from just how powerfully he was speaking. It was effortless.

What the doctor couldn't see was how special he was to me. All of the conversations we shared, our daily talks, sometimes about nothing, sometimes about basketball, or work, or the girl he had just gotten serious about. That doctor couldn't see how much Joseph had grown up this last year of his life, how he was putting things together after dropping out of college, how he was poised to become a real success if he had been able to continue working with his dad a little while longer. He once apologized to me on his Facebook wall. "Sorry for dropping out of college," he wrote. "But I promise I will graduate this life with honors." He was determined to do so (and he did).

To pass the time, all of us began telling stories about Joseph—to make him come alive in that room they had given us to wait things out.

"Remember   Jeff's   50th   birthday?" Someone said.

Smiles and laughter all around.

"Wasn't Joseph's speech the best?"

"The funniest."

"So kind and sweet," Another said. " 'I'm not just your son—' "

" 'I'm also your biggest fan,' " Brandi chimed in, imitating Joseph's words to Jeff.

"Cheesy and funny." We all laughed.

That event was the first time Joseph really opened up about how much his father meant to him in a speech to all of his family members. How much he admired him. I turned to Jeff. There was so much he still wanted to teach him. *Would he ever teach him anything again?*

"Joseph loved working with you," Jasmine told her dad.

"He said it was an honor," added Brandi.

A funny memory came to my mind, so I shared it with the others. "One day Joseph came home, and he was so happy. He was like a little kid. His dad had given him a raise. You remember that, Jeff? He was like, 'If Dad continues to give me money like this, you know how much I'll have? I'll be rolling in it!' I am going to make more than Brandi and Jasmine one day."

Joseph had his way of competing with his sisters. He used to tease Brandi that he was going to get married before she did. And Brandi hated the idea of that. It was all in fun though and he knew it. He just said it to get under her skin.

Everyone grinned at Joseph's innocence, his sweetness. Jeff the most. He loved Joseph so much. That was his boy. His son. "He had only gone from making $7 an hour to $15," Jeff said. "But you would have thought it was a million dollars more."

We couldn't help laughing. Then Brandi told a story of how Christian told her God was going to heal Joe. This inspired me to write on a nearby blackboard in our lounge, "Joseph is healed."

Yes, this what I wrote. But then a moment later, the dread crept right back in as that steel door leading to 312A opened and the doctor stepped out. I leaned into Jeff, bracing myself.

Remember to breathe.

Chapter 2: Disbelief

Disbelief: An inability or refusal to accept that something is true or real.

I had to get away. I locked myself in the claustrophobic bathroom far from Joseph's bedside and let memories of him and all the things he had said and done, big and small, flood my mind. Every day he would rub my stomach, call me Big Momma or some other nickname he happened to come up with from a television show, movie, or from who knew where. He had those moments where he could be so sweet to me … he would touch my hair, hug me tight or say, "I love you Mom. Can I have a hug?"

Tears filled my eyes now as I remembered these things and I whispered an adamant, "Lord, I will *not* bury my son."

And I heard Him reply, "I got him. Keep believing."

Bolstered by this new support, I returned to my husband's side in Joseph's room. Swallowing hard, I looked down at Joseph, motionless in the hospital bed, surrounded by monitors and hooked up to all of the tubes and wires. I reached for his hand. He seemed so serene, lying there as if he was about to open his eyes at any moment and call me Big Momma again.

Leaning down, careful to avoid the wires, I kissed his forehead. Already, most of me knew that Joseph would never wake up, never come back to us, never talk to me again. Yet, a sliver of hope remained. This sliver meant I could never give up entirely, especially with His words echoing in my mind, urging me to keep believing. *But believing in what?*

In spite of the tension raging inside of me, the day dragged on and on. Long periods stretched out where nothing seemed to happen, interrupted by a nurse entering to check a monitor or replace an IV bag. Every now and then an alarm would beep and a nurse would come rushing in. My breath would catch in my throat as I watched her glance between Joseph and the machine, pushing first one button, then another until the beeping stopped.

The shred of good news was that Joseph was still alive. Still with us. Still with Him. I could breathe.

Sometime later the alarm sounded again, once again bringing the nurse rushing to push the buttons.

"I set the monitor to be a little less sensitive," the nurse explained after seeing the worry on my face. "It's going off whenever the IV drip slows but it doesn't need to happen so often."

I smiled back at her, grateful for her humanity. Such a simple thing but an important one. She was including me in the conversation, making me feel like I was still part of Joseph's struggle.

As the night wore on, Jeff and I stood on either side of the bed, staring down at the unmoving form of our son, glancing at each other, saying little.

What can be said at such moments?

Meanwhile, friends trickled in one at a time, limited by the doctor's orders not to have too many visitors at once.

"How are you holding up?" one would ask.

"You okay?" another would say.

"Anything I can do?"

"Need anything?"

"I'm sorry."

Different words, kindly put, always meant to help. Yet, still just words. Nothing to fix the problem. Still, it seemed like every visitor offered the same suggestion: go home, get some rest.

"No," Jeff told them.

"No," I said.

I could tell Jeff wished to stay as much as I did. Neither of us wanted to be absent if—when—our son woke up.

Looking at Jeff's tired face, I guessed at his thoughts. My poor husband. *The fixer.* The guy everyone turned to make things right. He hoped this could be just one more problem he could solve, like the difficult legal issues he handled so well for the Players Association or the athletes who found themselves in trouble. I put my hand in his as I shared his hopelessness. We were both staring down a different order of problem, something far beyond even his competency. *What do work and money mean when your 22-year-old son lies in a coma? What does* anything *mean when all of your life's hopes lie in tatters, pieced together by tubes and wires and beeping machines?*

Despite our desires to remain, exhaustion caught up with us. Hours after the sun had set, I knew we had hit the wall. Jeff's eyes were shot with red, his clothes rumpled. Always put together, he looked so much older, as if a lifetime had passed since we got here.

And I could only imagine what I've must have looked like. Equally spent.

"Please," someone said. "Go home. There's nothing more you can do."

Our friends promised to call instantly if anything changed. Even though I felt my feet carrying me, my mind was somewhere else. Stuck in this terrible dream. Jeff kissed Joseph's forehead and I did the same, reaching for his hand, telling him how much I loved him. More tears fell as I said goodbye for what must have been the 10th time. Then the dream led me home.

Once inside our bedroom, more unreality surrounded me. Sleep wouldn't come. Lying in bed, all of the terrible thoughts struck at me. If being in a hospital was bad, being away was worse. I kept anticipating a call would come. Someone would reach out, telling me I missed something important.

I wasn't there.

The same dread must have afflicted Jeff. Catching his red-rimmed eyes staring up at the ceiling, I put my hand in his and turned to him. We whispered to each other in the dark. We prayed into the empty morning, reliving memories as if playing them back would strengthen Joseph's fight—as if doing so would remind Joseph his mom and dad were pulling for him.

The next morning, we arose early, saying little as we grappled with the enormity we faced. We returned to the hospital still in a daze. When all you want to do is cry, even talking is a challenge. As we exited the hospital elevator toward the tiled hall to the ICU, I prayed Joseph would be awake. I knew it was unlikely, maybe even impossible, but still, I hoped he would greet us. Before entering 312A, we said hello and managed smiles for the friends who had spent the night or just arrived.

Then Jeff and I took deep breaths and entered Joseph's room.

He looked lifeless. When I touched his hand, it was cool to my touch. *Where was the nurse? Why wasn't the beeping going off now?*

I raced into the hall to find a new nurse I hadn't seen before.

"Why aren't you by his side?" I demanded.

"I ..."

I didn't let her finish. "You're not doing all you can."

"I assure you, Mrs. Fannell, we are."

"The other nurse never left his side."

Beep! The alarm went off. Yet, she still didn't move.

I lost it. "The second that alarm went off, the nurse yesterday came running. She adjusted whatever needed adjusting!"

"I'm doing everything that needs to be done," the nurse assured me as she strode past to re-set the monitor. The beeping stopped.

I didn't believe her for a second. More could be done. More *had* to be done. The nurse checked another monitor and the IV, then left the room.

I turned to look down at my son, my anger melting to sadness. "Joseph, you can hear me," I whispered, leaning in close to his smooth, placid face. "That's enough now. You can open your eyes. Please, open your eyes."

I began to quote words of Scripture about healing and the promises of God. "You shall not die, Joseph," I whispered. "You shall not …"

My prayers went on as more hours passed with Jeff and me at his bedside. Nothing happened. Joseph's condition did not seem to change at all. At last I sought the waiting room for a break. After speaking with loved ones, I returned to room 312A with my sister, Liana, and her husband, Richard.

Moments later, the neurosurgeon entered wearing a white lab coat. After giving us a wan smile, he told us he needed to perform three tests. "These will determine … Joseph's chances."

Jeff and I looked at each other. This was it.

"It'll take a few hours, so if you could please leave the room."

The walking dream swept Liana, Richard, Jeff, and me back to the waiting area. More small talk continued with relatives and friends. Time passed slowly, slowly. Relatives of other patients came and went, some returned happier, others returned looking more somber than when they left.

At last the doctor arrived. Jeff and I scrambled to our feet, following him back to Joseph's room.

"The tests are complete," The doctor began, his face blank, his voice low but clear. "I'm sorry, your son is dead."

As if across from a great distance I heard Jeff wail, his face contorted in anguish. Liana and Richard walked in, slowly, hesitantly, crying, clutching each other, trying to hold on.

"Should I get the girls?" Liana asked, words that barely registered through my grief.

I said no, but she asked again.

I said no.

Again, she asked.

"We have to go get them." *Did I actually say these words or were they just in my head?*

I realized Liana hadn't heard me. I was floating outside my body, unable to do or say anything. Realizing this, I forced myself to breathe. Carefully, slowly, I breathed. At last, with great effort at control, I re-entered my body. I hugged Jeff harder and longer than I ever have, his eyes scrunched tight to hold back the tears even as mine flowed down my cheeks.

Hearing these doctor's words, my son had finally died and so did my heart. I stopped living and felt as if I never would again. I pulled Jeff closer to comfort him. Neither of us could form words. All I could do was think, "This wasn't supposed to be, God. *You said you had him.* You said to keep the faith."

God, it seemed, had failed Joseph and me. In this instant, I realized that since I couldn't rely on God, I had to be the one to shelter my family from this pain. As Jeff continued sobbing, I broke out of the dream, grabbing my life back. Willing my heart to beat for Jeff, for Jasmine, for Brandi, for Joseph.

Jeff and I summoned strength from each other and without a word, walked out to tell the news to our girls and all the loved ones outside. No one was immune from the anguish. Men I had never seen cry, broke down. Women I had never seen show more than a hint of emotion, screamed. I had seen Jeff, as pastor of our church, comforting grieving relatives. I thought I understood what loss was, but nothing prepared me for losing my son. So much sadness frightened me.

Worried my heart might burst from my body, I hugged onto relatives and friends. Beating wildly now, my heart felt as if it was fleeing to escape so much pain.

But then it all changed and I felt a peace I knew only God could give me. When it happened, my heart locked right back into its proper place.

"I got you," He said. "Breathe. Just remember to breathe."

As I comforted my husband, daughters, relatives, and friends, those were the very words I spoke to all those who had loved Joseph Malik Fannell, and all those who have come to me since that awful day, distraught and broken over their own loss.

Breathe. Just remember to breathe. Inhale, exhale.

Chapter 3: Depression

Depression: Feelings of severe despondency and dejection; a common and serious medical illness that can negatively affect how you feel, think and act.

Jeff and I were standing in our bedroom talking about funeral preparations. My 10-year-old grandson, Christian, was with us, too.

And then I saw him.

Standing in the entryway to the bedroom like he had so many times before. Joseph. My son. Except he was only 3 years old.

I screamed and ran to him, "Joseph. My Joseph!" He smiled up at me as I hugged him close. "Oh, my baby."

But Jeff and Christian didn't move. They just stared at me, bewildered, wondering what was wrong with me.

"It's Joseph. *You don't see him?*"

Jeff looked at me like I had gone crazy. "No. Where is he?"

"He's right behind you."

I turned to Joseph. "Joe," I said, "be still so they can touch you."

I wanted them to see him. I walked over to where Joseph was, gesturing, outlining his form where he was sitting on our bed with my hands. Jeff turned and looked. He couldn't see Joseph, but somehow could still feel him.

None of it made any sense.

"Why can't they see you, Joseph?"

And just like that, he disappeared without a word.

A moment later, he was back. Only this time, he seemed just a little older, like he was now maybe 5.

"Mommy!" he shouted.

I rushed to hold him. It felt so good to have him in my arms. Time disappeared. Everything else slipped away as the two of us held onto each other, both of us crying —

"Peach!" Jeff yelled, using the nickname I've always been called.

"Grandma!" shouted Christian.

"What are you doing?" They both seemed to ask at the same time.

"What are you holding on to?" Jeff asked.

"Joseph."

Just like before, they couldn't see him, but I could. And so I kept talking to him, touching him, squeezing my little boy.

"I miss you so much, Mommy," Joseph told me. "Heaven is so beautiful. Just wait and see." Then his voice broke and tears slid down his cheeks. "Mommy, I want you to come with me."

Without meaning to, I began shaking my head.

"But I want you to. I want you to come to heaven with me," he said, his voice rising.

"I can't," I said, tears pooling in my own eyes. "It's not my time to go."

"Come to heaven, Mommy," he begged, pulling on me to go with him.

Oh, the way it felt to hold him! He felt the same as he did all those years ago. I wanted to leave with him more than anything. I wanted to go. But I stopped myself. "No, Joseph. I can't. I have to wait until it's my time."

"Mommy it *is* time. I want you to come back with me. I don't want to

leave you again." Tears poured down his face, falling off his cheeks, sliding toward the floor as he clung to me. "I miss you, Mom. So much."

I couldn't stand to watch him suffer. It was tearing me apart. "Joseph, I miss you too. So very much."

Then his expression changed, and he simply said, "Die now."

I stood still—shocked by the words I just heard. Then he said them

again. "Die now, Mom."

Something about my expression must have caught Jeff's eye because he

came over and began shaking me. "What's the matter? What is going on? What do you see?"

"Joseph ... he wants me to go to heaven with him. He's crying."

Then Joseph said, "Kill him, Mommy. We can all be together."

Somehow Jeff must have heard him, because he yelled, "That's not Joseph. He wouldn't say that!" He looked me in the face, trying to reason with me. "Peach, this is crazy. Joseph did not die as a baby. He was not a little boy. He was 22 years old. Don't listen to him. That's not Joseph."

I turned back to Joseph, speaking in my sweetest voice. "Mommy can't come with you now."

My tone didn't matter. Joseph grew angry, scratching and hitting me. Frightened, I held him back, trying to prevent him from hurting me.

"Grandma, what are you doing?" asked Christian, looking frightened.

This made Joseph angrier. "Why are you listening to him? He's not your son. Listen to *me*, Mommy."

Jeff fell to his knees, praying, and a voice called to me from somewhere I couldn't see. "Rebuke him. You are the only one who can do it. Jeff cannot see him. You must do it. Cast the spirit away from you."

I reached out to Joseph, calling after him, wondering what I should do. Here he was, my little boy. My sweet child. My only son. *If I could only just hang onto him a little longer … If only I could just have him back. If only …*

I woke up crying in my bed.

It was morning—yet another morning without my Joe.

~~~

The date of my son's funeral was June 12, 2015. But I buried him on June 5, 2015. The day the doctor told me my baby was dead.

The day my heart died.

So, when I walked into that huge church the morning of June 12, and sat down in the front row with Jeff, Brandi, Jasmine, and little Christian, it wasn't really *me* sitting there. Or at least, not the me that had sat in a church so many Sundays before. This was a different person. This was *a mother who had lost her child.* I could see it in the eyes of every single person who looked at me. The helplessness. The pity. Nobody had ever looked at me this way before.

Still, I did my best to treat the day as the celebration of life my happy, fun-loving Joseph would have wanted. We all wore bright colors, as if we had put on our Sunday best, or had come to church on this warm, end-of-spring day for a wedding instead of a funeral. Most of the men wore bow ties for Joe and some of the women did, too. And while we all smiled and tried to looked cheerful on the outside, it had little to do with what was happening on the inside of every one of us. And my heart felt it.

The service began with video of Joseph speaking, presenting poems and participating in spoken-word events. This was his passion. And my reaction was almost automatic. For a brief moment, hearing his voice again, seeing him healthy and whole again, instead of hooked up to a bunch of wires and tubes in a hospital bed, my heart filled with joy. I knew on some level it wasn't real, but I couldn't stop the flood of happiness, the rush of relief that it was all okay, that Joseph was still here with me.

Then, just as quickly, the feeling evaporated. And that horrible emptiness came back as my heart broke all over again.

I don't know which part was hardest to hear. Listening to my child happily declare "every day above ground is a good thing," not knowing that in just a few months, we'd be putting *him* in the ground? Or when he talked about his family—about how much he loved his sisters, how his father taught him to be honest, and how I was always there for him, calling me his "lighthouse"—almost like he was saying goodbye without knowing it. When he said, "When I die, speak of me as I am ... with nothing false," the words felt both real and unreal. *"When I die ... "* How could my child, my beautiful, 22-year-old child, with his whole life ahead of him, have *died?*

After the video, some of Joseph's friends spoke to the crowd, and told funny stories about my son that made everybody laugh for a moment, even me. Then it was our turn. We rose together as a family and faced the roomful of mourners, people who had traveled from as far as Colorado and Missouri to bid farewell to my Joseph. I looked out at their faces, but they were all a blur. It was warm outside, but the room was hot, and the smell of fresh flowers was overpowering. I felt like I might faint and grabbed Jeff's shoulder to steady myself. None of it felt real.

Was this really happening?

Jasmine's voice crept in and brought me back to life. She shared funny stories of how she tormented her little brother—dressing Joseph up like Michael Jackson or stealing his Xbox controllers and leaving behind a hostage note. Once again, everyone laughed at the memory of my son, and I couldn't help laughing too, until the pain stole me back. When Jasmine concluded with a poem about when great souls die, I blinked back tears, barely able to hold it together.

Then it was Brandi's turn. She talked about how her brother called her "Momma Brandi," because she was 12 years older, and how Joseph was a "gentle soul" who was especially close to her son, Christian.

Oh, Lord, Christian. Hearing his name, I glanced at my grandson and saw that, like me, he was struggling to be brave, to not cry. I tried to give him a smile that said, "It will be okay. We're in this together. We're gonna make it."

Then it was my turn.

How does a mother stand and face a roomful of people—friends, relatives, acquaintances, even strangers—and talk about her son who has died for what feels like no earthly reason? How can you even survive something like that? I had no idea, but I knew I had to get through it for my girls, and Jeff, and for Christian, and especially, for Joseph. What kind of "lighthouse" would I be for my family if I lost it?

So, I steeled my nerves, and when I read a poem about how much I missed my son, my voice only faltered a few times. I talked about the day of the accident—it was agonizing that he was on his way to his father's office determined to finally start his life as a young man—when the other driver ran the red light and destroyed any chance of that. I only broke down when I talked about the relationship Joseph had with Jeff, his hero, role model, and protector. Jeff was just like the character John Quincy Archibald in the movie *John Q.* He, too, would have held a hospital ER staff hostage just to get a heart transplant for his son. Only there was nothing Jeff could do to keep our child here on Earth.

Up there in front of the crowd, I struggled to find words to make people understand how unique and special Joseph was, what the world would miss now that he was gone. How in our church, every time he spoke to the congregation, he never said, "Praise the Lord," like everyone else, he just smiled shyly and said, "Hello." Some people smiled at the memory, but their smiles didn't bring me joy. And when I reminded them of how, once Joseph started speaking, all the shyness evaporated and confidence filled him—it reminded me that my son who loved to speak had been silenced. I would never hear that voice, gaining confidence with each word, ever again.

And then I was done. I couldn't look at the people in the church, I couldn't face their helplessness and their pity. Instead, my knees buckled, and I fell into the arms of my family.

Jeff was the last to speak. Hearing the man I love say goodbye to his youngest child—his only son—was my breaking point. While I held it together outside, on the inside, tears ran like rivers down my face, as Jeff quietly but steadily (unlike me) remembered the day of Joseph's accident.

He said one particular story gave him hope beyond the grave, even though his heart hurt. You could hear a pin drop in the room except for the crying as Jeff explained he had been in Manhattan at a Major League Baseball Players Association meeting when he got the call about Joseph. All around him people tried to help. Someone hired a car. Then ex-major league pitcher Tony Clark walked Jeff out to wait for it. And while they waited, the 6-foot-8-inch Clark knelt beside Jeff, who is 5-foot-7½ in his tallest pair of dress shoes, and prayed with him.

Jeff's voice broke only once—when he told the crowd that as they prayed, he asked the Lord, "Save my son. Protect my son." He said the Lord replied, *"I've got your son,"* and Jeff said he knew at the time those words could be taken in one of two ways: either Joseph was going to be okay and the Lord would return him to us, or the Lord "had" Joseph because he was no longer ours. Of course, Jeff said, "I believed he'd come back." But when he learned Joseph was dead, Jeff said he remembered God's words: *I've got your son,* and so he gladly accepted what he heard when he prayed with Tony Clark. That God had his son. I wish I could have felt as accepting.

Then the whole terrible thing ended, and people hugged us and said goodbye and told us how sorry they were. Afterward, they brought us food, shared stories, and life went on.

But I didn't.

The problem with life going on is that it went on *without Joseph*. In his place, there was this almost bottomless feeling of pain. I drifted away from friends, my daughters, even my husband. No one seemed to understand what I was going through. I felt left out, like I didn't matter, like I was invisible. I turned to God, but even this didn't work.

Then, finally, I realized the truth. I was depressed. I had lost my son and with him, my courage and hope.

I know how hard it is to find the "right thing" to say or do when the unthinkable happens to someone you care about. I also know how hard it can be to deal with someone battling depression, like I did after I lost my son. It's hard to get through that wall of sadness. It can feel like the depressed person doesn't even want you around. But I promise you, if someone in your life is suffering, they *need* you. Not to make the pain go away—no human being can do that—but to help lighten their load just by being there during those darkest times. In fact, when no one reaches out, people who grieve wind up feeling ashamed of their emotions, like their pain is driving people away and they need to pretend to be okay. They can't share their pain, so they internalize it, which makes it even harder to heal.

At least, this is what happened to me.

And that's what I think that dream was about, when Joseph tried to convince me to die. Because that day was the first of many I considered the dreadful possibility. On one hand, of course I knew I wanted to live—I had a husband, two daughters and a grandson who needed me. But the pain was so bad. My heart hurt so much I could physically feel as if Joseph's death tore a hole in me. And I desperately wanted this suffering to end, to the point where I almost didn't care how.

That's how the devil gets in there—when we're at our weakest. He manifested himself in the dreams I had about Joseph and used my desire to end the pain to try to trick me into ending my life. Luckily, my husband, my daughters, my grandson, and my God made sure I always found my way back from those dark thoughts.

Even in my dreams, God reminded me to *live and to breathe.*

There aren't words to describe how devastating it has been to lose my youngest child. But I have learned and grown through the experience of grief, and one of the lessons I've learned is something I think applies in a lot of different situations.

It is okay *not* to be okay.

We're always striving for perfection in every area of our lives. But perfection is only possible in heaven. Here on Earth, it is okay to be imperfect, and it is okay to hurt. Sadness is not a failing in you or in God. Remember the father of the boy with the unclean spirit who said in Mark 9:24, "Lord, I believe but help my unbelief." Grief is a sign of how much you loved the person you lost.

While sharing grief might not always feel comfortable, studies have shown burying grief is worse. It causes depression. I know this too well, because I buried my grief and wound up depressed. Lord, I know how powerful sadness is—how it can get inside of you, robbing you of any chance to enjoy other parts of life you once loved—a sunrise, the sound of laughter, songs you used to sing in better days. Think of all the famous, successful people who were deeply loved, like Robin Williams, Bobbi Kristina Brown, Kate Spade, and Anthony Bourdain, who took their own lives. And for every name you know, there are so many more you don't.

That's why I believe it's better to talk about grief than to hide it. Pretending is not living. Don't be afraid of being labeled a "drama queen" if you share your emotions; drama can be a call for help, or at least for someone to listen. It is okay to tell someone about your pain and grief. When all is not right in the world (or at least your part of it), it's okay to feel bad, to be sad, to mourn and to grieve. It is okay to display your emotions—*all of them*.

In the Bible, when God commanded Ezekiel not to mourn his wife, there was a specific reason for this command. Unless God Himself specifically tells you not to mourn, I'm telling you to go ahead and mourn. Because it is okay *not* to be okay. It is also okay to say you are not okay. Continue to believe. Continue to have faith. Continue to ask your friends, your family, and God to help you with your struggle.

And one day you will be okay.

How do I know this? The day Joseph died, I buried my heart. Then God gave me something—something I desperately needed so I could continue living for Jeff, for Brandi, for Jasmine, for Christian and for me: *a new heart.*

So, I admit it—I am not okay, not even now. But I know someday, I *will* be.

Chapter 4: Hope (Will He Rise Again?)

Hope: A feeling of expectation and desire for a certain thing to happen.

It was the same thing every morning.

The sun would peek through the window, and my body would start to wake up. I'd feel the warm sensation of being snuggled in my bed, blankets all around me. And as I came into consciousness, my body would start to tingle with this feeling of expectancy ... almost an excitement. I'd be flooded with intense relief, that it had all been a bad dream, that I was waking up from a nightmare, that I'd walk out my bedroom door and life would be the way it used to be...

And then I'd remember. Joseph's not here. And my heart would sink.

For some reason, I could not get my brain to accept the fact Joseph was gone. Of course, there were moments when I knew, usually the moments when I'd cry uncontrollably, or when my heart would ache with emptiness.

But I soon discovered a new way to cope with my reality.

I hoped.

I had hope that there was a good reason God took my child from me. I hoped He was using Joseph's death for His glory. I actually began to believe my son would soon be raised from the dead. After all, the Bible is full of stories of people who are dead one moment and alive the next. Jesus raised people from the dead. Lazarus was risen after four days. Elijah lay on a little boy and the little boy was made alive. Dorcas was risen from her death bed by Peter. Jairus' daughter was "awakened from sleep," as Jesus called it ... the list goes on and on. *Why couldn't one of those stories, those testimonies, be mine? Why couldn't Joseph return to us?*

I was going through life like a mother who lost her child, but inside, every cell in my body was waiting for God to resurrect Joseph, bring him out of the grave, *wake him up.* I listened for my Joseph's voice asking, "What's for dinner?" Or for Jeff excitedly calling, "Peach! You'll never believe who's here!" I looked around corners expecting to see his beautiful smile. I told myself that I had to believe. So I believed. I cried out in prayer, "God, you've done it before. You can do it again."

I was hoping *hard.*

When my hubby reminded me of the Scripture that says, "Many days later there arose out of the grave," it only strengthened my hope. "Surely, God, you can do this for Joseph," I prayed. If I just hoped and prayed and believed hard enough, my son had to come back to me.

But he didn't.

Weeks went by, yet there was no miracle. And the more days passed without God raising Joseph from the dead, the further it felt like my child was slipping from me. *Would I forget what he smelled like? What his voice sounded like?* I found myself replaying moments from Joseph's life, trying to put the pieces together of the puzzle that was my son. Trying to burn every aspect of who he was into my memory so I would never completely lose him.

I flashed on Joseph as a little boy, in the backyard of the house we rented in Virginia. He was so happy out in the yard, playing by himself for hours on end, with bugs, with cars, with rocks or whatever interested him. I used to love watching him play video games with his sisters and his dad, everybody trying to beat each other, yelling "Take this with you," a line that I have come to love to hear so much. It reminded me of just how much they enjoyed playing this particular video game.

But the one image I could not get out of my head was 2-year-old Joseph staring intently at the VCR, rewinding the movie *Jurassic Park* over and over again to watch his favorite scene. I think I've seen that scene—the one when the kids are in the car and the dinosaur leans over and they all scream—at least 600 times.

That's because *Jurassic Park* remained Joseph's favorite movie long after he started watching it all the way through. Attending the premiere of the latest *Jurassic Park* movie became a family tradition. In fact, when a new *Jurassic Park* movie premiered shortly after Joseph's death, Jeff, Brandi, Jasmine, Christian, and I all piled in the car and went to see it in his honor.

And it wasn't just about the movie. I'll never forget seeing the look on my son's face one Christmas as he opened the box that contained a set of *Jurassic Park* action figures. Pure joy. The toys, which he referred to as his "men," immediately became prized possessions. As he got older, I'd occasionally go through his room to get rid of things he had outgrown, but he never let me dispose of his "men." One time I forgot and added the action figures to the giveaway pile. The next thing I knew Joseph was digging through old clothes and toys and random junk in a valiant (and ultimately successful) effort to rescue his "men" from destruction. Today, they stand guard in Jasmine's condo in Chicago, serving as a constant reminder of her brother.

When we first moved to Columbus, New Jersey, Joseph met the boy who would become his closest friend, Anthony Rodriguez. He was our neighbor and our families became close as we watched our boys grow up together. They'd play all day, sometimes with Joseph's "men," sometimes outside, and it seemed like one was always sleeping over at the other's house. I still laugh thinking of the night they went "camping" in our backyard and, in the middle of the night, suddenly came running back in the house in a panic when some noise spooked them.

Other memories would stir in me as I remembered the story of Joseph's life. How in junior high, Joseph's other passion was basketball. He wasn't much of a player, but the boy could shoot. He used to call me outside to watch him make shots, even while blindfolded—because he was that good, and he knew it. Especially at those three-pointers he passed down to his sincerest admirer: Christian.

As soon as Christian was big enough to shoot a basketball, Joseph made it his mission to train his nephew to be a basketball star. He'd challenge him to a game every time he came over, and Joseph was so serious about his role as "coach" he would not let Christian come in the house until he determined Christian had enough practice for the day. Even now, Christian loves the game and promises that one day, he will be in the NBA. He especially likes to take three-pointers, just like his uncle taught him.

I can't help thinking how life was good like this for years—until Joseph entered high school. Suddenly, something changed, and he became a little withdrawn and angry, too. Out of the blue, he'd explode and yell at me or one of his sisters. It was so unlike the sweet boy I knew. I wondered what was going on. His dad worked in the city and sometimes got home late or had to be away overnight sometimes. Was Joseph angry about that? I often wondered.

I wouldn't learn the truth until Joseph turned 20 and we sat down for a heart-to-heart talk one day about the things he wanted to do with his life. That was when he told me he had been bullied as a kid. It hurt me to hear how others would sometimes make fun of him—how even his best friend Anthony couldn't stop it. However, high school was also when Joseph discovered a way to silence his critics—or at least gain power over all of the kids who called him names: Spoken word poetry became his passion.

"Spoken word," as it's called, is a form of poetry in motion. It doesn't necessarily rhyme, but it definitely has a rhythm. And Joseph was great at it. I think that's why Joseph gravitated to spoken word in the first place—it made him stand out, in a positive way. He won accolades from his peers and attention from teachers and administrators, which made him feel good about himself, something he needed so badly. And, of course, nobody made fun of him when he was performing. He was too good at it. After being bullied and feeling like he didn't fit in, delivering spoken word made him feel liked— like he finally belonged.

Spoken word also gave him an art form he could use to express his feelings about the pain he and so many kids experience when they're bullied. He shared his story with eloquence and passion, letting kids who were going through what he went through know they were not alone:

> *I never been in the military,*
> *but I got this Purple Heart*
> *I got it for beating up on myself*
> *for things I can't fix*
> *I learned to hate myself*

at such an early age,
I wrote "God doesn't love me"
  on the inside of all my notebooks …
…Depression can guide people
  to very hollow places
Places where flocks of vultures
  lurk on things that I find beautiful
And often I ask myself,
  "Am I beautiful?"

Writing and performing spoken word was a natural evolution for Joseph. He'd been writing stories and poems ever since he was little. I remember him coming to me as a teenager wanting to develop some tales he'd written back in elementary school, but my computer crashed, and I lost them. Luckily, I still have notebooks full of his writing in his room.

One day I was in the kitchen making dinner, and he walked up to me and said, "Mom, do you think remembering is a talent?"

"Why?" I asked him. I had no idea what he was getting at.

"Listen to this," he replied. And then he recited a poem, word for word, with a rhythm and style that made it more like a *performance* than a recitation.

I was amazed. "How did you do that?"

"I don't know. I guess I just … felt it."

"Well, of course that's a talent. That's a *gift*."

I was so proud of my son at that moment, I thought my heart might burst. Not many people can recite a poem from memory at all, let alone in rhythm.

I didn't realize it then, but this was the beginning of Joseph's spoken word career. He started memorizing pages and pages of poetry, then he'd test them out on me. For example, we'd be in the car and he'd suddenly say, "Mom, listen to this one," and perform a new poem. He was practicing, refining his craft, getting better all of the time. Then came the day he got to demonstrate his new skills at our church talent showcase. I watched my son take the stage and perform before the congregation. The audience was captivated— all eyes were on him, on my Joe, watching in awe. Then, when he finished, he walked over to me and gave me the biggest hug.

That was a good day.

It's funny how things work. In real life, Joseph was normally so shy and unassuming, but that all changed completely whenever he was performing. Onstage, he was confident. He was sure of himself. He was funny. He was proud. Whenever he performed, this little smile would light up his face right afterward, as if he knew people were loving what he was doing, and more importantly—loving him for doing it.

As he got more and more into spoken word, he started performing at other churches in our area. Teachers would invite Joseph to come to their classrooms to show their students what spoken word was all about.

What a difference time makes.

Growing up, Joseph's peers didn't get him. That's why they would make fun of him. But once Joseph found his gift, all those younger kids in school came to admire him, to look up to him the same way little Christian did. They loved his visits and Joseph saw a great future for himself in spoken word—he was even talking about performing on a cruise ship. He loved the stage and the stage loved him. He belonged there, just like he said.

But things don't last. Especially it seems, some of the best things.

When Joseph got to college, life changed again. The opportunities to perform he'd had in high school dried up and some of his shyness crept back in. And since Joseph went to college with a lot of the same children he went to high school with, old patterns began repeating themselves. Some of these same kids—now young adults—would talk about Joseph behind his back. They began excluding him from group activities. Hurt and angry, he left them all behind—even Anthony. He began spending more time alone in his room playing video games. Occasionally, he'd head out to the driveway to shoot hoops like he did in junior high and high school. But mostly he kept to himself.

In the months after Joseph died, I found myself wondering about Anthony, why he and Joseph drifted apart. How he had been doing since Joseph had been gone. I talked to his mom and she said Joseph's death hit him hard, to the point where he struggled to even talk about it. She told me that every day, Anthony wore the green bracelet from the New Jersey Sharing Network, which we were given for donating Joseph's organs.

Originally, I had been skeptical about organ donation. My baby had just died, and now they wanted to cut him open? But the organization had asked if we would consider donating Joseph's organs and we needed to make a decision quickly while they were still "viable." When Jeff, Brandi, Jasmine, and I talked about it, we came to a decision to donate. Joseph's organs wound up saving the lives of five people, a miracle that made us proud in spite of our suffering.

In addition to Anthony wearing the bracelet, he guarded the bow tie of Joe's he had worn to Joseph's funeral, refusing to let anyone touch it or even the funeral program. (My Joseph loved to wear bow ties!) Shockingly, about two years after Joseph's death, Anthony went into the hospital complaining about a headache and never came home. He died June 10 from Adult-onset Still's Disease (AOSD), just two years and five days from the day Joseph died. He was our neighbor, he was Joseph's friend and he was only 24; the same age Joseph would have been.

~~~

Anyone who knows me knows I love to take pictures. I don't care much about being in them, but I will take them at the slightest opportunity. The birth of my grandson, Christian, was the perfect (albeit involuntary) model. We had just celebrated his ninth birthday and I found myself watching videos and looking at some of those pictures. As I was reflecting on him, God brought something to my remembrance. I had journaled about it when it happened on October 6, 2011.

I had received a call from my daughter, Brandi, asking if I could please pick up Christian at school. My grandson, who was 7 at the time, had been complaining of stomach pains but she was at work and couldn't get him. I brought him home, but when he was still suffering after a couple of hours, I looked in his eyes and made a decision. It was time to take him to the hospital.

We arrived at the ER around 2 p.m. By 9 that night, numerous tests had been performed, but the doctors said they were all inconclusive. Maybe it was his appendix? They weren't sure. By that time Brandi joined us, they told us we had three options: Christian could go home with Brandi watching him to bring him back if necessary, Christian could remain in the hospital for observation, or he could be transferred to another hospital with a pediatric unit to run more tests.

Hearing this, Christian started to cry. "I don't want to stay in the hospital. I'm not in pain anymore. I want to go home!"

The doctor left us to make our decision.

Brandi turned to me. "What should I do?" she asked.

"You're his mama," I replied. "You need to make the decision. Just follow your heart."

Brandi immediately said, "I want him transferred."

Christian broke into more tears, crying louder than before. Now Brandi was unsure and looked to me for help. As I tried to figure out what to say, Christian suddenly blurted out, "Did anybody ask God? Did you, Mom?"

Surprising us all, he declared that he would ask Him what to do. He closed his eyes to pray. Then he opened them. "God said I'm going to be all right. I want to go home."

I had no idea what to do. While Brandi continued to comfort her son, I left the room and called Jeff, who said we had to do what was best for Christian. I realized that, as Brandi's mother, I had to help her find the strength to stick with her decision. Christian was transferred despite his tears. He spent the night in the hospital and, after no more pain, was discharged early the next evening. The doctors never determined the cause. Bless God.

Now as I recall the days following this incident, I find myself returning to Christian and how brave he was. But what really stood out was the way he expressed his faith. When I first brought him home from school that day, I had prayed for him and when the pain wouldn't go away, he wondered, "Why isn't it gone, Grandma? We prayed. Why didn't God take it away?"

What I realize now is that Christian had hope, just like I had hope that God would bring Joseph back to me. His hope and his faith in God gave him the expectation that God would end his pain. And later on, when we had to decide, Christian was the one who asked, "Did anyone ask God?" He knew God had the answer and God told him he would be all right.

But God never said *when* he would feel better or that Christian could go home. Through the lens of watching Christian's experience, through witnessing Anthony's equally senseless death, God has allowed me to see faith is about asking the Lord for direction, for healing, for whatever it is we need.

Hope means having the expectation that He *will* answer. Maybe not on our time table, but eventually. Expectation is hope. "Hope maketh not ashamed. God will answer." We just have to believe this—we have to *know* this with the faith of a little child—just like little Christian.

Which brings me back to the point when I lost my hope. That's when God reminded me of the real meaning of the Scripture that I so easily tossed back into His face. The Word says hope maketh not ashamed. Our expectation *is* that hope. And our expectation, our hope must be in God, based on the Truth of His Word. "For when the trumpet sounds, those who are dead in Christ, shall rise and we shall be caught up to meet the Lord in the air."

One day Joseph will rise again, and so will I. That is my hope. That is where I must place my hope. That expectation. And that is what I will hold onto as I remember to breathe.

Chapter 5: Loneliness

Loneliness: Sadness because one has no friends or company, (of a place) the quality of being unfrequented and remote; isolation.

As the weeks dragged on, the hope I had been clinging to faded. I did what I thought I was supposed to do. I hoped and prayed and believed. But God had not performed the miracle of raising my son from the dead. He did not bring him back to me.

It was starting to become clear He had other plans for Joseph.

My ears no longer strained to hear the sound of my baby's voice, practicing the rhythms of his latest spoken word piece in his bedroom down the hall. I stopped half-expecting to walk into the kitchen and see him standing at the refrigerator, scanning the shelves for leftovers to munch on. And the hardest part? I stopped waking in the morning with the warm (but fleeting) feeling of relief and anticipation, before reality set in.

Because in my heart, I knew there was nothing left to anticipate. Joseph wasn't coming back. There would only be one person in the house in the late afternoon: me.

In place of hope, new, uncomfortable feelings snuck in. Anger. How could my son be taken from me at such a young age, when his life was just beginning? Why was Joseph in that place at that exact moment? Why did that driver run that red light? Why couldn't the doctors do something to save him? Frustration. Why *my* son? What did he do to deserve to have his life cut short? He was a good person, a believer in the Lord who tried to do right by everyone he met. He was going to be somebody. He mattered. He was *loved.*

Worst of all, I began to lose my belief in the One who said He can do the impossible. Because He didn't do it for me. He didn't do it for Joseph. I had believed the Scripture "hope maketh not ashamed." I had made Scripture the center of my life, hoping and praying with my whole heart and soul, *believing* the Lord would make it all okay.

But nothing happened. And in the end, my hope made me feel shame.

The shame came when I shared my feelings with some of my believing friends. These were people I trusted, people who loved God just like I did, so I asked them the questions in my heart. Why didn't God raise Joseph from the dead? Why did *my* hope mean nothing? I wasn't questioning their faith, I just needed their help. Nothing made any sense to me. The God I believed in would not have done what He did to me and my family. He would not have taken our baby away. Maybe they could help me understand …

But when I expressed my feelings to these friends, some of them didn't offer support, much less sit with me and just listen and let me share my pain. The words out of my mouth—the mouth of a woman of faith—actually shocked them. Who was this angry, questioning person? How could she say such horrible things? *Where was her faith?*

Just when I needed them the most, people started moving away from me as if I had a disease. And all of a sudden, I found myself in a place called Loneliness.

I had so much pain inside, but no one to express it to. No one to help me navigate this journey called grief. Sometimes the pain hurt so bad I felt like it was going to rip me in two. It was overwhelming. I couldn't live with it, but I couldn't get past it. I was just stuck with it. So, I sat down and wrote my thoughts and feelings out, pouring my pain onto the page, hoping somehow I could make sense of the waves of anguish battering my heart and my soul.

"It's been five Fridays since we've buried our son Joseph," began one of my entries. "And it's been some kind of roller-coaster ride. Every passing day new questions arise. Why, Lord? How could You allow such a thing? It wasn't supposed to end this way. And as each question gets ignored, seemingly, another question surfaces. But no matter how many questions, I ask, there are still no answers. There is only silence."

I stayed locked inside my mind, writing and searching for answers, as if they were hiding in some corner of my brain. As if had I found them, it would all make sense. My imagination worked overtime, coming up with all the ways it could have been so different. Playing out the scenarios of what would have, what could have, and what certainly *should* have been. A career, maybe even in spoken word, bringing his message to people all over the world. Then marriage. Then grandbabies who would look up at me with the same beautiful smile. ..

But it isn't going to be. Not ever. And life goes on as I scramble to pick up the pieces ... in silence.

As the days go on, I write and I write and I write because I have to express myself—

because I have to get this get this hurt out of me. Even if no one's listening.

> *22 years old he was.*
> *Just realizing his purpose.*
> Silence.
> *The dreams, the visions,*
> *the promises You made.*
> Silence.
> *Friends have come—*
> *some who we thought were not.*
> *Some who we believed were—*
> *only to discover hidden plans and* *agendas,*
> *promises made and broken.*
> *It's something to find out you*
> *do not mean to some what*
> *you thought you did.*
> Silence.
> *So many emotions.*
> *How can you be so high on life one day,*
> *only to hit rock bottom the next ...*
> Again. Silence.
> *How can you be surrounded by so many*
> *at one time, never feeling alone,*
> *never left alone...*
> *not for one solitary moment...*
> *and become virtually invisible the next?*
> Even more silence.

How can it be silent, and yet be so *loud*? In the beginning, when we first lost our baby, I remember it was just loud. There were days when the phone rang so many times, I felt like we were living in an emergency call center, even though the emergency had already passed. But those calls didn't stop the pain. It's still here—even more than before.

So why the sudden silence? And why so loud?

Nothing has changed. He's still gone, and we still have no answers. There once were notifications *and more notifications*, back to back. Buzzes. Vibrations. Dings...constant and consistent.

And now...just silence.

I'm yearning for the rings and dings and buzzes that only come every once in a while. I long for human contact. The sense that somebody, anybody, can understand what this is like. Or at least cares enough to help me through. Not that I know where "through" is, or how to get there.

In a way, I do understand, on some level, why people disappear after tragedy strikes. They know they can't heal the pain. They know they don't have the words to make it better. They feel helpless and powerless in the face of such an awful thing and the profound grief that follows. Losing a child is against nature. It isn't supposed to happen. And since they can't make it better—since they can't make the pain stop—they do nothing. But what they don't realize is how much more it hurts to be left in silence. As if anything could hurt more than losing my Joseph already does.

I'm trying to find some new sense of normal, holding onto those few things in my life that feel routine, part of my old life, before my heart was ripped out.

Then one day, it occurs to me if I do the things I used to do, maybe I can escape the silence. Thinking this might help, I throw myself back into life. I go to the salon, sit in the chair, get my hair done, make small talk with the hairdresser. I treat myself to a manicure and a pedicure, choosing my favorite color from the rows of bottles of polish. I push the buttons on the massaging chair and it feels good, those vibrations down my back. I go to church, sit in the pew, listen to the familiar voice of my husband, the preacher, (amazed at how he still does it) speaking the Word, as I have so many times before.

So simple.

And for a moment, like those mornings back in those early weeks when I woke filled with hope, life feels familiar and sane. I feel like myself. But only for a moment. Then reality screams in my ear. Loud. "Things *are not* the same. Things will never, ever be the same!"

That's what I mean by loud silence.

I try to run away from it, but it doesn't matter. I still hear it. No matter what I do, how far I try to run, I still can't escape. It follows me. *And when I manage to slip its grip, even for a moment?* It beckons me. Calling out my name. "I'm still here," it says. "Don't you hear me?"

Of course, I do. It may be silence, but it's deafening.

Answering it, I hold on. We hold on. We still have each other, I think. Always have, always will. Wasn't that the way it was? Then I'm reminded. We still have each other … until we don't. That's when the questions come flooding back like a dam breaking in my heart and my head, letting everything I try to hold back in, all in one moment.

But still, there are no answers. Only more silence. Silent, yet so very loud. "Why are you screaming at me?" I ask.

Even now as I write this, I realize it doesn't make sense. How can "loud silence" exist? Isn't that an oxymoron?

Not always. Sometimes, the loss of something in your life leaves a hole so big and raw, its absence speaks louder than its presence ever did. Joseph's voice was soft. He was a quiet person. He did not call attention to himself, except when he was on the stage, performing. But the absence of his quiet voice is like a thundering waterfall in my head. Pounding its message into my soul. "He's gone. He's gone. He's gone."

In absence, there is silence. Talk about deep calling unto deep. The silence is speaking so loudly, so deep sometimes I can't hear myself think.

> When will it end, Lord? How do I go on?
> *Silence...still.*
> *Still silent?*
> *You answer...Be still.*
> *Be still and know I am God.*
> *You are God.*
> *But I still don't understand, Lord.*
> *How did You make me*
> *to contend with horses,*
> *but I can't contend with silence?*

I knew I was in trouble when I tried to go shopping several days later. If there's one thing in the world I love, or at least used to love, it's shopping. But even this didn't do it for me, didn't take me out of this dark place. Walking through a mall packed with people, talking, laughing, living their lives, all I heard was silence, still.

And it was so very loud.

Be still. You said again.

Still your heart. Still your mind.

That is where I am.

Remember Elijah and how he looked for Me.

It was silent for him, too.

I am God...And I am in the still small voice

of your silence.

Wait for Me there. And hear Me.

It's not so loud where I Am.

And it's not so silent.

I never felt more alone than in these first months when I realized Joseph was never coming back. I could hear my tears echoing back at me as they rolled down my face. That's how silent it was.

While it hadn't been very long since we'd lost our son, it seemed like an eternity. How long had it been since I'd heard him laugh, since he wrapped me in a bear hug? My body ached to hold him again. It felt like he'd been gone forever, but at the same time, like he was here just yesterday. It was the strangest feeling, like I was frozen in time.

But to the crowds that had been calling and texting and checking on me, time had definitely moved on. Forget about even the occasional ringing and dinging and buzzing. That ended. Now, there were no more texts or phone calls or knocks at the door or deliveries of flowers or "Call me if you need me."

The very same people who had offered their sympathy and the standard "Anything I can do, just let me know" seemed to have forgotten our names and our address. "Yes, you can do something," I screamed at them in my mind where I took them to task. "You can *be* here for me! You can *care*!" But except for a small, handful of friends I could count on (and for whom I will be forever grateful), there was no one. And of course, I said nothing.

It was a time of loneliness. A season of solitude. Quiet. Harsh, loud quiet.

So, even after the uncomfortable trip to the manicurist—even after the depressing shopping excursion—I still tried to find comfort in the mundane. I still tried to escape the silence by going out some more—to fix these feelings within me. Out there in the world, where people were living their normal lives doing normal things, maybe I would feel normal too?

But wherever I went, even in the middle of summer, with kids on break hanging out in groups or walking with their parents, and people going to and from work and doing their jobs, and people socializing with friends, I only heard more silence. That and my ever-present tears, and under that, the echo of my own heart beating. Sometimes I could hear it pounding—beat, beat, thump ... beat, beat, thump. It sounded like I was holding on for dear life.

Maybe it was trying to remind me *I* was still alive.

Then one day I found myself standing at a checkout counter, buying something. The cashier looked up at me, and words came out of her mouth...

"Credit or debit?"

I just stared, blankly. I didn't hear the words. Instead, just by asking a simple question, she somehow jolted me back to reality. It meant remembering my Joseph. Remembering he is not here. And won't ever be again. Soon, anything and everything seemed to remind me of this fact—something I'd almost overlooked in my struggle to be normal and relate to others again.

I'd be someplace later and hear a mother talking to her child. I'd see a boy shooting hoops on a playground. Even watching a bird flying across a bright blue sky triggered this realization. No matter the impetus, no matter the trigger, the message stayed the same: "Your Joseph is gone."

And every single time, it felt like a punch to the stomach.

Even at home, where no one could puncture my bubble or say something to elicit these thoughts, I found I couldn't escape. Then the silence would roar louder than ever before. Chasing me. Torturing me. It followed me from room to room, from morning till night. The silence of my house without my son in it. It was a rude silence. A horrible silence. And I hated it. Lord, I hated it more than anything I had ever known.

That's when I became bitter.

Chapter 6: Bitterness

Bitterness: Sharpness of taste; lack of sweetness; anger and disappointment at being treated unfairly; resentment.

Imagine you're a soldier on a battlefield. All around you, rockets are exploding, bullets are flying, and people are yelling orders you can barely hear. It's like you're in a movie, only it's real life, and you've never, ever been more terrified. Even though it's so loud your eardrums hurt, you're so scared you can still hear your heart pounding. It feels like it's going to burst out of your chest …

And then it happens. You get hit. You lay there, perhaps in pain, perhaps in shock as the battle rages around you. There is more yelling and people rushing everywhere. It's total chaos. But part of you is calm. Because you know one thing in your heart.

Your fellow soldiers are going to get you off the battlefield.

"Never leave a man behind" is the soldier's creed. No matter how badly wounded somebody is (or even if they've died), no matter how much work it will take or how dangerous it is to remove them, they will not be abandoned.

I grew up thinking real life worked the same way. Friends and family? We had each other's backs. We held each other up when the chips were down. We gave each other a shoulder to cry on when we needed it, without judging. There was no way we would *ever* abandon one of our own in the middle of one of life's battles. Until I was the one lying there wounded.

Maybe I hadn't been shot or hit with a grenade, but Joseph's death wounded me—so deeply there were times I wondered how I didn't die from the pain. I could feel it physically, like my heart really had been ripped out of me. In its place was an empty, hollow ache. It felt like I was being stabbed. Sometimes it was so bad it made me double over in agony.

And the worst part was, in my mind, this pain came directly from God. He was the One who hurt me, who tore my heart out, who took my baby away from me and did not bring him back no matter how hard I hoped, believed, and prayed. The One I had complete and total faith in, whom I believed in with all my heart, had cut me to my core.

It was almost like I lost my son and God at the same time. Worse, when I was at my lowest, my "fellow soldiers" left me behind. They deserted me. And this filled me with more bitterness.

Maybe my anger at God frightened all these people away. Maybe they had no idea what to say to me or how to help. Or maybe they were just ready to get on with their lives, even though I could not imagine ever getting on with mine again. Whatever the reason, I was alone. I spent hour after hour by myself in the house where Joseph used to be, where he used to fill my afternoons with sunshine. (You really never know just how much you miss someone's presence, until they're gone). Meanwhile, everyone else went on with their lives.

As Christians, we like to say, "We are soldiers in the army of the Lord" like the song sung at just about every church in America:

> *I'm a soldier in the army of the Lord.*
> *I'm a sanctified soldier in the army.*
> *Got my war clothes on,*
> *in the army of the Lord,*
> *got my war clothes on,*
> *in the army.*
> *If I die, let me die,*
> *in the army of the Lord...*

It's a great song, don't get me wrong. It empowers you. It gives you strength and courage knowing you're part of an army, which means you have some backup. You have brothers and sisters to help you in your fight. To help you in your Christian walk.

Lately though, I have seen some forced to walk alone. And I'm not only talking about what happened to me. People I know have fought the good fight of faith, holding on while dodging life's blows. Most of the time, they've remained victorious. But then comes a blow so massive and powerful it knocks them to the ground. I've seen everything: people losing loved ones, suffering financial setbacks, enduring health crises, experiencing hardship of all types, including some tragedies I can't begin to fathom.

What I do understand is the blows. When they get started, they can keep coming at you, making you feel like you're a boxer in the ring just trying to make it through to the next the round. The struggle is to hang on as blow after blow rains down on you. I've seen people shaken to their core who have stumbled but have not fallen, despite unbearable suffering. Of course, I've been impressed by their resilience. We all are. "Isn't she amazing, the way she keeps going?" Someone might say. "Isn't he a rock?"

But some people *do* fall. They take blow after blow, hit after hit, until they reach the point at which they just can't take any more. And they fall to the ground like wounded soldiers. Down for the count.

Does this make them less worthy? Does this make them less good? Just because they can no longer withstand the pain and maintain their cheerfulness, their hope, their faith in God? They've failed the test, they've failed to endure like Job, so they're just out?

Sadly, it seems some people feel this way, leading them to walk away from other wounded souls just as they walked away from me. They abandoned my family and me, stranding us in enemy territory. Because that's where you are when you're left behind without your faith. You're in the devil's clutches—vulnerable to whatever temptations might come your way.

I wanted to know if my thoughts about soldiers and battlefields even made sense. So many thoughts were swirling around in my head, and it was hard to keep them straight, so I turned to one of our church members who happens to be in the military, and asked him, "When a fellow soldier has been wounded, what is the right response?"

He looked at me quizzically, as if he couldn't comprehend my question. Then he answered, "They don't *ever* leave them there. They don't leave them alone. Soldiers go back and they pick them up, even if it means the threat of losing their own lives. They don't even think about it."

"But even if it's dangerous?" I asked.

"Yes. Because it's a dishonor to their country and their fellow men and women to leave them there."

How about that? A *real* soldier knows we are all in this thing together. If you die, we all die. A true ally says, "You can count on me. No matter what. I got your back."

I believe it ought to be the same way with us in the battle of life, especially with our fellow Christians. Like the song says, aren't we all soldiers in the army of the Lord? Aren't we all in this thing together? Shouldn't we have each other's backs?

Still, it doesn't matter what your faith is, if you see somebody hurting, can you really say, "It's not my responsibility," or "I don't have time to be depressed," or "I got my own issues going on?" Really? Will you just continue to fight your own battle, while your brother or sister lies wounded on the field? Or will you risk your life, your happiness, your comfort level, the space you're in, the things you know—and think you know—to go and pick him up?

I believe this is something we must all ask ourselves. Am I my brother or sister's keeper—or not?

If we are all soldiers in the army of the Lord, shouldn't we all be fighting the same enemy, or at the very least, making sure our own comrade doesn't get lost in the battle? Ultimately, if this person loses, you do, too. Allowing another to perish, leaving them behind, does not honor our great human family.

More importantly, what I have learned is this: Today it may be your brother or your sister hurting, but tomorrow the person left wounded on the battlefield may just be *you*. And if or when that happens, will the brother or sister you left stranded take time out of their busy life to pick *you* up?

I certainly hope so, but they would have every reason to strand you in the same way— unless we *all* take up the mantle and truly fight for each other, unless we all make other people's suffering the same priority as our own. What grief has taught me is that I'm a soldier in the army of the Lord, for real. And I got all my brothers' and sisters' backs.

For I know better than anyone now—if you lose, I do too.

~ ~ ~

Before Joseph died, we had so many friends. People were always inviting us places—to events, over to their homes for dinner or out to lunch. Not that they were around us all the time, but sometimes it seemed like they wanted to be. I never imagined it could be any other way.

But in those weeks and months after the funeral, as I spent my days walking in the shadow of grief, those friends who couldn't get enough of me simply vanished, like a magician waved his magic wand and made them all disappear. And let me tell you, it *hurt.* On top of the unimaginable pain of dealing with the loss of my child, there was this new, unexpected wound. *Were these people really my friends at all?* I wondered. And if they were, why didn't they care enough to be there for me?

In time, I came to see they certainly weren't soldiers in *my* army. Of course, they were all there at the funeral, packing the pews, sharing hugs and kisses and promises of help: "If I ever needed anything." At the time, it felt like they had my back, and I expected they would continue to. After all, there had been so many promises.

But only a couple of weeks after funeral, these very same people began vanishing from our lives. Now, months have passed since I lost my son and the phone that once rang all day long remains silent. No one ever appears at my door with a cookie, let alone a meal, or because they "just happened to be in the neighborhood." As for invitations? Nothing. No one invites us anywhere. I suppose we wouldn't have been much fun at a party. Still, it would have been nice to be asked.

Bitterness has consumed me so much lately. I am genuinely disappointed by my friends' behavior. I didn't expect this after losing a child. Especially not from those people who were supposed to be in my faith family. I am a wounded soldier, and no one cares enough to help. Instead, they just pass by me on life's battlefield. And the longer I lie, the more bitter I feel.

As you might expect, much of my bitterness is directed at the driver of the car who ran the red light, causing the accident that took Joseph's life. After an investigation, the Burlington County Prosecutor's Office determined that while the driver had "disregarded a red light," they were not going to prosecute him.

This only added to my bitterness.

Knowing we wouldn't receive any justice from Burlington County and the state of New

Jersey for Joseph's death, we decided to sue the driver in civil court. I wanted everyone to pay for my pain, but especially the man responsible for taking my son. We hired a lawyer who filed a suit stating the driver's conduct was "beyond simple negligence and demonstrated indifference to the safety and welfare of other motorists, specifically Joseph Fannell."

The case began. But the problem with lawsuits is, you talk about them and little happens for a long time. Lawsuits also dredge up painful memories. There are so many facts to remember, different offices and people to deal with, and about a million questions to answer. All these little details swelled inside my brain, feeding my bitterness. And even though I knew what I was doing was right, sometimes, I didn't want to think about lawyers, judges, or the jury anymore. I wanted to think about my son.

But apparently, on this one day, at a particularly low moment for me, Jeff happened to be thinking about the lawsuit, too. Even though he tended to not speak of Joseph as his way of coping, today he was discussing the lawyers and the prosecutor's office, and the reporter who didn't say enough about Joseph in the newspaper article.

And then he asked me a question.

To be honest, I have no memory of what the question was. It could have been as simple as, "What did the attorney say?"

Whatever it was, I just *snapped.*

All the bitterness and anger I'd been holding inside of me came pouring out in what I can only describe as a torrent of ugliness. I didn't want to say the things I said. I knew they were terrible, awful words, but I couldn't stop.

I remember the look of shock on Brandi's face as this stream of bile came out of my mouth. I remember Christian, lying on the floor, pretending as hard as he could to be preoccupied with whatever he was doing on his cellphone, staring at his screen, not daring to look up at me. Only Jeff, who had started the whole thing by asking a question, responded in his calm, unshakable way.

"Don't get mad at me," he said. "We're all in this together."

What caused me to lash out, not just at the friends who abandoned me, but the people I loved the most? Looking back, I think it was three emotions all rolled up into one: bitterness, anger, and frustration.

Luckily, Jeff's voice brought me back to reality. Right afterward, I saw the tears in my daughter's eyes. I noticed my grandson panicking in his spot on the floor. And I heard my spirit say, "Breathe."

"Give me a moment," I told them all. Then, I forced myself to get it together, to just breathe, as I had been for all the months since the accident. Remembering to breathe had been getting me through.

"I know we're all in this thing together," I finally said when I regained control. "Whatever just came out of me, I didn't ask for it, and I don't like it, and I'm sorry. I'm sorry I lashed out at you all."

In one brief moment, it all made sense. I realized just how frustrated and bitter I had become in the months since Joseph's death. *Was this who I was now? Was this who I would be forever?* I hoped not. And I determined in my spirit, at least in the moment, it was time for me to let those feelings go. After all, I still had *my* army. Jeff, Brandi, Jasmine, and Christian were my loyal soldiers—my troops. And no matter what happened, they would not leave me on this battlefield alone. Just like I would never leave them to suffer.

We have each other's backs. Always and forever.

Chapter 7: Sadness

Sadness: An emotional pain associated with, or characterized by, feelings of disadvantage, loss, despair, grief, helplessness, disappointment and sorrow. An individual experiencing sadness may become quiet or lethargic and withdraw themselves from others.

There's a famous book called *The Shack* by the Canadian author William P. Young. The book is about a man who loses the youngest of his three children in a terrible tragedy, just like I lost my Joseph in the car crash. It's also a book about pain. According to the author, the title is a metaphor for "the house you build out of your own pain." I now understand this pain—the pain of a parent who has lost a child—all too well.

This is probably why, in the months after I lost Joseph, I read *The Shack* over and over again.

What was I looking for in those pages? Maybe the book helped me feel less alone, like there were there were other people out in the world who suffered the same kind of loss I did, went through the same grieving process, and somehow got through it. Maybe it helped put words to the emotions I was feeling and made them easier to process. Whatever the reason, I was obsessed.

Perhaps my obsession with the book had something to do with the fact the story also offered hope. As he moves through the healing process, the narrator gets help from God, Jesus, and the Holy Spirit—*in person*. Maybe, I believed, this meant there were better things in store for me if I just hung in there. Perhaps if I continued to walk my walk and trust in the Lord, it would all make sense someday.

At this point in my life, however, the only part of the book that made sense to me was "The Great Sadness." This is the term the narrator uses to refer to the loss of his child. Oh, how this term spoke to me. But unlike the narrator, I had not (yet) run across any members of the Holy Trinity during my grieving journey. However, I understood The Great Sadness fully and completely because it was what had enveloped my heart, my soul, my life.

My personal Great Sadness began a few months after we lost Joseph. Up until then I had been experiencing a roller coaster of emotions—the shock of the news, the inability to force my brain to accept it was true, the bitterness regarding my disappointment with family and friends—until finally, I was consumed by the loneliness and depression surrounding my new life as a Mother-Who-Lost-a-Child, alone in my empty house, feeling like an outcast from my former self.

Each of these emotions fully consumed me when I was going through them. But eventually, they all evaporated like steam from a teapot.

What I was left with was the sadness.

I think the sadness snuck in when there was nothing left to distract me. I was no longer angry or bitter at the world, or at my friends who had been uncomfortable with my anger or had otherwise moved on with their lives. I had given up hoping and praying for Joseph to be risen from the dead. I finally knew in my heart my child was gone and he was not coming back. There was nothing to do except go back to my normal routine in my empty house. Which was the hard part. The empty house.

Everything in my home, the place I loved, made me think of Joseph. Whatever room I walked into, I'd be reminded of something he said, something he did, something he liked. I missed him tremendously, like I'd lost a part of myself. Which, I suppose, I had. And hard as I tried, I could not get used to living there— or just living, period—without him.

It was kind of strange actually, because, it wasn't just us in at that home, initially. It was US. It was me and Jeff and Brandi and Christian and Jasmine and Joseph. It was ALL of us. Then it became four of us – Jeff and me and Jasmine and Joseph. And then, for the past four years or so before his death, it was just the three of us. Three of us in that house. But it still felt like home. It still felt right. It still felt like US.

I had to stop cleaning certain rooms and doing certain tasks at certain times. For example, Joseph always came home in the afternoon when I was in the middle of either cleaning the shower or changing our bedroom sheets. Whichever activity brought its own special ritual. I'd be down on my knees, scrubbing the tile in our shower, only to be knocked over by a giant bear hug coming from behind. No matter how many times he knocked me down, he'd be back to do it again a few days later, and we would always both end up on the floor, laughing.

Laughter aside, I much preferred the times he'd walk through the door when I was in the middle of changing the linen. Without fail, he would join me in the bedroom, grab the other half of whatever sheet or blanket I was working on, and help me make the bed. With his help, the job was so much easier, it took me half the time, or even less. Plus, it was something we shared. It was one of our rituals.

I miss those rituals. To this day, I still can't fix the bed or clean the shower without half-expecting Joseph to walk in the bathroom and knock me over, give me a kiss, or help me out in the bedroom. So, I don't do those chores anymore. They've become too much for me. It just brings the sadness back. And I've learned in this journey to stay away from things I know will cause me pain.

The sadness also came unbidden whenever I would walk into Joseph's room, which, of course, I happened to do every day. It was my son's room after all. His stuff was still in it. Going in there was a way to feel closer to him and to remember. I'd touch the bed where he slept, the twin size bed that he never wanted to graduate from even though his legs hung over the edge for years, because he liked that bed. Sometimes I'd smooth the blankets, even though no one had rumpled them for months. I'd open the curtains to let the light stream in, even though there would never really be light in my baby's room again. At least not the kind of light I wanted to see.

And every time I walked in, the sadness overwhelmed me. It felt like there was a hole in my heart where my child used to be.

If you've never lost a child yourself, it might be hard to understand what I'm describing feels like. There was a time when I didn't know this pain like the back of my hand. Losing a child is like child*birth* because you can't really know what it's all about until you experience it. But childbirth, while definitely painful, comes with a major upside. It brings joy, not grief. And it's also a part of nature. The world is working the way it's supposed to work when you bring a child in the world to take care of, who will someday take care of you.

Losing a child is the opposite experience. It goes *against* nature. As parents, we aren't meant to bury our babies, we are meant to raise them up to be good men and women who will eventually bury *us.* Sometimes I found myself wondering if we humans just aren't biologically equipped to lose a child.

It's strange, because my own mother knew (and still knows) this same pain. She has buried four children—one at just a few months old, and then three more, including two in the past three years. Her strength amazes me sometimes. But apparently, I did not inherit that strength, because there were moments when I felt like I could not survive the pain. I couldn't believe it hurt as much as it did in so many ways. Pain overtook my entire body to the point where I thought I might die.

So, what does it feel like to lose a child? The pain is so deep, it's like you've fallen to the bottom of a waterless well. You're way, way down in this cold, deep, dark pit, and when you look up all you see are stone walls rising in a circle all around you, blocking the outside world except for one little circle of light. And the walls are so high, there's no way climb out into the light. It's like you're trapped.

But the pain has a physical side, too. Sometimes it feels like the sharpest knife you can imagine, cutting you to your very core and taking a piece of you with it. There have been times when my heart hurt so bad, I swore I could *feel* it, like I was bleeding, even though nothing had so much as grazed me. Or I could feel the emptiness inside of me, and the emptiness hurt. Even though, as far as I knew, my heart was still in there. It had to be. I was still alive. I was still breathing.

This pain, and my Great Sadness, wasn't limited to the space inside my house. As I've said, sometimes, I would try to drag myself into the outside world and away from what felt like the source of the sadness. But no matter what I did—go to a movie, shop, attend church, or pray to the Lord to take my pain away—the sadness followed. It felt like it would never end.

Then came the day I hit bottom.

I walked into Joseph's room like I had so many days before. Smoothed the bed. Opened the blinds to let the light in. And I was flooded with a very specific memory.

In our family, we had (and still have) a ritual of praying for each other whenever one of us leaves the house. Every day before Joseph departed for work or school or just to go out, he would come over to me, wherever I was: on the couch in the living room, at my desk near the front door, in my bedroom. When he came to me, he would bend down and put his head in front of my hand, where I could reach it, or sometimes, he would take my hand and place it on his forehead. In both cases, it was so I could pray for him.

This ritual of praying for each other started many years before and became a way of life for our family. Even little Christian, at the time, still made sure we prayed (and sometimes prayed himself) before heading out the door and into the world.

That day in Joseph's room, my mind flashed back to a moment when we came home from church. It had been a funny kind of day. Joseph wore all white to church, and wow, did he ever look sharp. It had to be a special occasion, I think it was Mother's Day. Anyway, we got back from church, parked the car in the driveway and got ready to walk in the house through the garage like we always did. That's when we heard it:

Buzz buzz buzzzzzzzzzzzzzzz!

Oh, Lord. Our garage was swarming with bees! (They still tend to build hives around our house, for some reason.) Almost instinctively, Jeff and Joe stopped heading for the door at the same moment and took off after the bees. They managed to chase them all away while I just stood there and watched, dumbfounded. The funny thing was, my phone happened to be recording while they were chasing the bees. I had no idea at the time, but I got to hear all the drama of their encounter later on.

When the men finished chasing the bees, we all walked in the house, and the conversation again shifted to how sharp Joseph looked in his white suit. I looked him over and remarked, "Dad would never wear white."

Joseph just laughed and said, "I bet you he will wear white on my wedding day, if I want him too." Then we were all laughing, and Jeff finally agreed if it meant so much to his son, he *would* wear a white suit. Just for one day.

Joseph got a kick out of that.

Then Joseph realized he was hungry and wanted something for lunch but needed to go out and buy it and didn't have any money. However, he did have a check he needed to deposit anyway, so he decided he'd go to the ATM and take care of everything. And just as he was about to leave, on this very average, everyday errand, he walked over to me in the kitchen, bent down a little because he was taller than me and said, "Pray for me."

I put my hand on his forehead. I closed my eyes and prayed to God. "Lord, keep my Joseph safe as he goes."

I was remembering all of this in Joseph's bedroom. And that's when it hit me. The day Joseph left the house to drive to his father's office, the day the man in the other car ran a red light and took everything away from me, I had not been home to pray for my son. I did not send him out of the house with God's blessing, the way we always prayed for everyone in our family.

I let him out there *alone*.

If my brain had been working logically, it would have realized I hadn't been home all week and Joseph had been fine for most of it. The accident did not happen on Monday, the first day I was gone and had not laid my hand on Joseph. He had gone out every morning without a prayer from me and nothing happened—meaning it wasn't my prayer keeping him safe. Maybe it made him feel safe, but God was keeping him.

Until that day.

But months later, standing there in his room, remembering Joseph looking sharp in his white suit, joking about his father and his wedding, and sending him out the door with a prayer like it was the most natural thing in the world ... it hit me hard. I had failed to pray for my baby and now my baby was gone. The sadness came crashing down on top of me like a wave.

I collapsed on top of Joseph's bed and cried a cry I don't think I'd ever heard come out of my body before. It was so loud I'm sure the neighbors could hear me if they were home. It was the sound of a wounded animal. All the sadness that had built up inside me over all those months, I never let loose. I had been trying to hold it together, trying to focus on other things, trying to move on with my life like I thought I was supposed to.

Until it finally exploded out of me, right there in Joseph's bedroom in the middle of the day. The unbelievable, unbearable Great Sadness came over me, and my tears rolled like a river. I wailed and wailed until the wailing subsided into sobs. Then I lay there trembling for I don't know how long. Minutes? Hours? I'm really not sure.

Because the next thing I knew, I had fallen asleep, there on my son's bed, in the room he would never return to. Just like a baby will fight sleep, crying out until it's exhausted, and then finally fall asleep—I cried to the point of release. My body was tired of fighting. My mind was tired of fighting. And maybe because, for the first time, I finally let go, I slept.

Chapter 8: Anger

Anger: A strong feeling of displeasure and belligerence aroused by a wrong; wrath; ire; grief; trouble.

One morning I woke up filled with anger. I wasn't even fully conscious, and yet my mind already raced, consumed with the unfairness of it all. *How could this be happening?* My son was gone, but the man who took him away from me was still here—still living his life as if everything were normal, at least as far as I knew. He still got to wake up every morning. He still got to talk to the people he loved.

He still had his life.

Yet we had heard nothing from this man who took our child. Not even an "I'm sorry." It's not as if he didn't know what happened. It's not as if he didn't know Joseph died, and that he was responsible for his death. But with the trial inching along and no verdict yet in sight, no one was holding him responsible. No one was making him pay.

So, I decided I would. I would write a letter to my son's killer. I called him a killer, because first and foremost in my mind, that's who and what he was.

I sat at my computer and typed furiously, rage pouring out of me onto page after page. I said things to the man who killed my son that I wouldn't want my friends or family members to read, ever. But I was so angry, so furious, and I wanted him to know it. I wanted him to *feel* it. I wanted him to give me an answer, to tell me why, because no one would. No one had an answer for me. Not even God. Which is why the man who killed my son wasn't the only target of my anger.

I was also angry at God.

I would kneel to pray just as I always had, but instead of prayer, all that came out was a series of questions: "How could you let this happen, God? How could you not stop it? You are all powerful—all-knowing. Why didn't you see this coming? Why did you allow this man to kill my son? Why did he get to live? Why did he get to walk away when Joseph couldn't? Why couldn't Joe just be paralyzed?"

You know you've hit a low point when you start bargaining with God, asking him to substitute a different, slightly-less-bad thing for death. Being paralyzed isn't life. Being comatose isn't life either. I wouldn't wish either of those things on my son, not that any of us had a choice in the matter. There were no choices. There was only the question: Why? Why? Why?

"Why did You not let me see him one more time?" I called out. "Why couldn't he say anything to us? Why did we have to see him like that? Why didn't the nurse take care of him the way she was supposed to? Why did You do this, Lord? Why, Lord, why?"

I began to seriously question my faith. After all, I had held up my end of the bargain. I lived a good Christian life, raised my children to be good Christians, and yet God took one of those children away from me. This did not seem at all fair, and I let God know I was displeased. "Some of those things You spoke to me have not come to pass," I said. "I prayed Psalm 91 over my children, my household, every day—and I believed that You heard my prayer. But Joseph still died."

How was I supposed to believe in this God who took my child away? In my mind, there was only one solution. I needed to hear from the Lord—directly. Sure, I could read His promises in His Word, but I wanted to hear it from His mouth. I demanded a personal revelation. His Word spoken, His Word coming to pass. A promise fulfilled in my life.

But God did not speak to me. There was no personal appearance. So, the "why" questions continued, even angrier than they had been before. "Why did we work for You? Why put our trust in You if You are not going to come through? Why pray? Why continue to ask You to cover my children, if you are going to let the worst thing that could happen to them happen anyway?"

Why were there no answers? Why did nothing make sense? I no longer wanted to talk to anybody, even my family, since every conversation I started always ended with anger, and more why questions. They weren't usually directed at the person I was talking to, of course, because what could they do? Only God could help me, so my anger and my questions were always directed at the Lord.

But here's the thing I didn't count on. It turned out God had questions for me as well. Questions like: "Oh, ye of little faith, why do you doubt? Why do you continue to kick against the goads? Why have you forsaken Me?" God answered my questions with questions of His own. And in that moment, He caused me not only to rethink my questions, but also to answer them myself. I saw what I had been missing all along—God was God and He was sovereign, and my only job was to believe Him. So, I did.

I fell to my knees and cried out to God, "I forgive You," and my anger faded. Since forgiving God meant accepting what happened, it meant I no longer had a right to be angry. I wrote a long blog post about what I learned during this process, which is included at the end of this chapter. I also rewrote my letter to the man who killed my son.

This is what I wrote to him:

August 13, 2015

To the Man Who Killed My Son,

I don't know what to say to you. I just know I need to say something, so let's start there.

It's been a little over two months now since the car "incident." I can't really call it an accident, since an accident is an unfortunate incident that happens unexpectedly and unintentionally. As far as I can tell from the police report, you ran that red light on purpose, intentionally, making a decision to change lanes to avoid a car that was already stopped so you could race through the intersection.

Writing to you is not easy. We've had your name and address almost from the very beginning, but I have not been in a place where I felt I could say anything to you … at least not anything kind. Instead, I chose to endure the silence, for a time. But while I waited, at no point did you reach out to us to express your sympathy. So, today, I decided to write to you.

Let me tell you about the person you hit when you decided to speed through that red light. His name was Joseph. He was a real human being. He was just 22, the youngest of our three children and our only son. He believed in God and went to church, where he was developing his ability as a spoken word artist. He liked to sing, draw, play video games, and shoot basketball. In fact, besides me, his dad and his sisters, Joseph also left behind an 11-year-old nephew, who he spent every spare minute teaching to dribble and shoot three-pointers.

And you killed him.

Joseph was on his way to work that morning, heading to the office where he had been working with his dad for the last year. He was so excited by the prospect of "working among lawyers," as he put it. He was filled with so much promise, just beginning to learn the tools of the trade.

He had so many plans for the future! He was planning to go back to his high school to perform spoken word, but also to talk to the students about bullying, because he had been bullied at school. But now he can't help those kids. Not only did you kill him, you snatched his dream away. You stole his future.

The day you hit him, Joseph took a different route to work than the one he usually took. I told him his dad always took Route 206, because it was easier. How I wish he did not listen to me that day. But he did. In my heart, I believe taking that route was just another way for Joseph to pay tribute to his dad. He wanted to be like his father even more than I knew. He was just beginning to show it, in little ways. But you took that away from us, when you ran that red light.

He always drove safely. He always wore his seat belt, and even though he was a young man and liked "muscle cars," as he called them, he maintained the speed limit. Unlike the stereotype of young male drivers, Joseph used caution and control behind the wheel. Unfortunately, no amount of caution or control would give him the ability to see you coming. How I wish it had! But it didn't. So when you decided to run that red light, you killed him.

I have a picture of that morning playing over and over in my mind, like a movie I can't stop or turn away from. I see Joseph *going through the roundabout to cross Amboy Road, on his way to work, thinking about what he would do once he got there, clueless as to what was about to happen. Then I see you and I wish I could somehow go back in time and warn Joseph to be careful, that you were coming right for him. But I can't. So you speed through the red light ... and ... SLAM!*

I see it every time I close my eyes and remember Joseph. Sometimes it even plays when my eyes are open.

He was on his way to work. It was not even 10:00 in the morning. He was three short minutes away ... and ... SLAM!

Cut off—from life, from me, from his family, from his future. You did that.

What were you thinking? What was going on in your mind? Were you distracted? Were you on medication? Were you supposed to wear glasses? Were you on your cell phone ... or even texting?

The red light was clear as day. I know because four of them go across that bridge, sitting just above the road so they can clearly be seen. How could you have missed them? All four ... really? Oh, how I wish there was a camera there. But my reasoning, and my own experience, tells me you had to see those lights. And when you did, you made a conscious decision to go through them anyway.

Do you have no awareness of what you did? You hit someone. You killed someone. It wasn't an animal. It wasn't a squirrel. It was my son. His name was Joseph.

He was 22. You are 74. You've lived your life. His was only beginning. The newspaper reported you walked away with "minor" injuries, not even enough to warrant attention. You actually decided to decline medical treatment. My son was not given that choice. He died.

And yet, for two months, you have stayed quiet. You feel no need to reach out. You don't express your thoughts, your sympathy. Maybe you don't feel any.

So, let me tell you what I feel. Every time—every single time—I need to go to the supermarket, in order to get there, I have to pass through that intersection. So every time I need a few groceries, I have to relive the longest nightmare of my life. I have to see the picture-that-won't-go-away of what happened in the middle of that intersection. I can't even go pick up some ice cream without being reminded exactly why my son will never cry out, "Don't forget the chocolate syrup, Mom!" again.

My husband also has to pass through the same intersection every time he goes to his office. It takes him less than 15 minutes to get to work. And every day, that same picture plays in his mind too ... SLAM! Plus, not only does he feel Joseph's absence at home, he feels it at work, too. Because Joseph lived with his father and Joseph worked with his father. And you took that away when you ran through that red light.

One morning as I prayed, I asked the Lord to cover my children ... and I accidentally included Joseph. Now every time, every day as I pray, I pause when I call out their names, reminded that one is missing. I can no longer ask the Lord to cover Joseph, because Joseph is not here. And then the scene in my mind plays again, and I suffer the pain all over again, and think of the pain my baby must have felt when you ran that red light and smashed into his car.

Yet you go on. Free. Able to walk the streets, to go to the supermarket, to cross that intersection, to enjoy your life, the holidays, your family, go on vacation and live out the rest of your days. While my son can't, and neither can we ... at least not like we did before. Not without the reminder. SLAM!

That's where it ends every time I remember Joseph. Good times, fun times ... SLAM! You killed him.

You have forced us to deal with a reality we did not sign up for. We certainly did not see this coming, any more than Joseph could see you, speeding into that intersection despite the light telling you to stop.

Honestly, I don't know why I'm writing to you. I guess what I want most of all are answers. Not that they would really make a difference, or any sense. But did you consider, at least for one moment, what it might mean if you ran through a red light? Did you hesitate ... even for a second?

Traffic laws exist for a reason. To protect lives. To protect somebody's child. When you broke the law, you took away Joseph's protection. When you made the decision to run a red light, you stole his life.

I really don't know what else to say to you. I want to hate you, but the love of God won't let me. I want so much to see you locked up, to make you pay, to make you suffer, to make your family suffer as we do ... but at the same time, it doesn't quite feel right. I can't say I want revenge, because it's not mine to get. And it won't bring my Joseph back. I know it won't.

But I do want justice. I want Joseph to be vindicated. I want your license taken away. In fact, I want every person who reaches the age of 65 (including myself, when I get there) to be tested every year in order to renew their license. As for you, I want you to be punished for the wrongful act you committed ... the reckless decision you made to speed through that red light. You chose to do it. You chose to break the law, and you need to be punished for your choice.

But most of all, I want to hear you say, "I'm sorry." You don't have a right to remain silent in this case. You owe us at least that much. You owe at least that much to Joseph.

But you know what? Even if you never apologize, I forgive you. Not because I want to, but because I have to. If I don't forgive you, I'll just be allowing you to steal another part of my life and remain silent while you do it. Then you will not only be the man who killed my son, but the man who continues to kill me, every day, by poisoning my heart with anger.

I can't say I expect to hear back from you. I don't even know if you'll ever see this letter. But I had to write it. For Joseph.

Sincerely,

Evelyn Fannell

Joseph was gone, and I still couldn't really understand the reason. But I also understood, "Why did Joseph have to die?" is one of those questions I can't know the answer to, at least as long as I'm here on Earth. When I get to heaven, I will ask God myself. In the meantime, God continues to speak to me in His own way. He tells me that not only is it okay to ask questions (as long as you're prepared for Him to ask you some), it is equally okay to ask why.

Soon after I wrote the letter to the man who killed my son, I also wrote the below blog as my way of cathartically releasing the anger I felt. It's my hope that it offers solace to those also have experienced grief and wrestled with their doubts.

Questions, Anyone?

In our walk with God, if we're honest, we can admit that we have our moments (albeit long ones sometimes) when we have questions. We were believing in God "for" something, waiting for a promise, expecting justice, and even found ourselves at a loss at unexpected turns. I certainly have experienced all of this, especially in the months since the loss of my son, Joseph.

This led to me asking God a bunch of questions. I still do, in fact.

We present our questions to God—"Why this?" "How long?" "What now?" And seemingly, we do not get an answer (and definitely not the one we want). In fact, God often leaves us with a question. In particular I am reminded of the many He asked of Job, starting with "Where were you when I created when I created the earth?" (Job 38).

In life, things sometimes don't pan out the way we think they should, leading us to ask our questions. We act foolishly, we pout (naturally and spiritually), and throw our spiritual tantrums. Then we host a pity party, inviting God, and anyone else who will listen to us, to complain.

And God in His sovereignty comforts us and allows us to groan and moan for a time, but then He shows us the error of our ways. And when we still don't quite seem to get it, He simply leaves us with a question, just as He did with Job, and even more so as He did with Jonah.

In case you are not familiar with the story of Jonah, Jonah was a prophet of God who was told to go to the people of Nineveh and declare the Word of the Lord, telling them that if they repented, they would be saved. But Jonah did not think the people of Nineveh were worthy of being saved.

Let me stop here. Some of us have the same attitude. We forget God has delivered us and saved us from some things—bad habits, bad attitudes, bad ways of thinking and doing things, sinful acts—meaning we were once considered unworthy, too. And here's a news flash: we still are, in and of ourselves. For it is by grace we are saved, not of works, lest any man should boast. That means in spite of us and who we thought we were, God yet saw fit to count us as worthy. Worth saving. Hallelujah!

But, like Jonah, we have this way of hanging condemnation over other people's heads, becoming judge and jury to what they have done or are doing and making them feel as though they are not worthy to be saved. Wrong! God saved you. He saved me (the wretched one that I was), surely, He can save someone else.

Okay, moving right along...this is where Jonah was. He believed the people were unworthy of God's deliverance. So instead of doing what God told him to do, Jonah figured he'd run. And so, he ran, right into a storm, which landed him smack dab in the belly of a fish.

Jonah ran away from what God told him to do. When he was instructed to go to Nineveh, he paid his fare on a boat that was on its way to Tarshish, which was in the opposite direction. Twice the Bible says, 'to flee the presence of the Lord.' Jonah must have thought that Tarshish was a place where God does not dwell. Some scholars believe the spirit of prophecy was evident in the city of Nineveh because God had work to do there, so when Jonah decided to flee, he thought he was fleeing from the spirit of God breathing upon him to go and preach the Word. What Jonah failed to realize is that if God tells us to do something, it doesn't matter where it is. God will be there.

We can't run from God. The psalmist David said, "Where can I flee from your spirit? Even if I make my bed in Sheol you are there. You are everywhere." (Side note—Sheol is a dark place that is considered to be hell. A place where evil resides, where evil is practiced.) On Earth, it's that place where you do your dirt. And God sees it. He sees you. From the minute details of lying, bitterness, and anger to the acts of lust, fornication, unforgiveness and murder (whose spirit did you kill with those judgmental words or gossip?). There is no hiding from God. He will always find you.

Don't forget He seeks and saves those who are lost (or even, in this case, hiding).

Anyway, back to our issue at hand. Being the forgiving God He is, God delivered Jonah and gave him a second chance to go and make it right. "Declare My Word to the people," God said, "that they may be delivered." This time Jonah obeyed and delivered the Word, a Word of warning to the people that their city would be overtaken. And after hearing the Word, the Bible says, "The people fasted and repented."

We have to stop here, too. What do we do when we receive a cautionary Word from a man (or woman) of God? Meaning, do we turn around (change our ways) or do we turn against them (the person delivering the Word), talking about them every chance we get? Do we get it right or leave the church? I'll just leave that one right there. That's between you and God. But God already knows...

Anyway, when God saw that the people turned away from their sins, He delivered them. But after He had done so, Jonah developed an attitude with God. The Bible says in Jonah 4:1-3, "But it displeased Jonah exceedingly, and he became angry. So, he prayed to the Lord, and said, "Ah,

Lord, was not this what I said when I was still in my country? Therefore, I fled previously to Tarshish; for I know that You are a gracious and merciful God, slow to anger and abundant in lovingkindness, One who relents from doing harm. Therefore now, O Lord, please take my life from me, for it is better for me to die than to live!"

Then God showed him an object lesson. God is always teaching us and causing us to see things from His perspective, molding us to be better. As Jonah sat pouting and angry at God for saving the people, God allowed a tree to grow to keep Jonah from the heat.

In the midst of our spiritual tantrums, God is YET merciful, as He was with Jonah. Then God allowed a worm to eat away the tree, and Jonah once again expressed his displeasure. So, God simply asked him a question, "Should I not have pity on them, as I have had on you?" and left Jonah alone. Hear the Word of the Lord: "Until you can answer God's question, He will not answer yours." For there the book of Jonah ends.

Many of us, myself included, have asked God many questions in times of suffering and confusion. We have our whys, hows, whats, ifs, and, buts. Excuses on top of reasons and reasons on top of excuses for why we can't or why we won't do something. And God, being the merciful God He is, does for us anyway. Provides shelter from the storm, makes a way of escape, delivers us, provides for us.

However, too often this is just not good enough for us. Oh, it serves us for a time. But we have short memories. Things don't go our way and we forget. There really is Truth in the Scripture, "forget not all thy benefits." For if we remembered them, we wouldn't ask so many questions. But we do, so I will say it again. Until you are ready to answer God's questions, He will not answer yours.

Have a question, ask it, but be prepared to answer first. Otherwise, you too, might remain in a place of anger longer than you would like.

Chapter 9: Functioning

Functioning: Working or operating in a proper or particular way; fulfilling the task or purpose of something.

Back in the '50s (before my time!), there was a hit song by the Platters called "The Great Pretender." It reached No.1 on the R&B and pop charts in 1956, still shows up in all kinds of movies and TV shows and is on just about every oldies playlist. So, chances are, even if you're a disco/original hip-hop girl like me, you know the song. Still, it came as a bit of a surprise when, in the middle of my morning devotional, the Lord spoke to me and said:

"You have been the Great Pretender."

Ouch. He was right (as He always tends to be, of course).

I was taken aback at first—but I've gotten used to the way the Lord has been speaking to me over the years, however mysterious it is. Then the Lord spoke to me again, calmly and clearly: "Look up the words."

So, I did. And this is what they said: *Oh yes, I'm the great pretender. Pretending that I'm doing well. My need is such, I pretend too much. I'm lonely but no one can tell.*

Well, that certainly summed it up. I was the Great Pretender. And I had been pretending for a long, long time.

***

When you learn somebody you respect or admire is struggling with alcoholism or addiction, your first reaction is often surprise. You had no idea they had a problem because they kept it hidden so well ... until they couldn't anymore. Every day, they'd get up and go to work, or drive the kids to school, or whatever it is they needed to do, and meet all their obligations.

But as soon as they got to a place where they didn't have to be someone's employee or boss or mom or dad or sister or brother—the second they didn't have to pretend to be okay—they'd drink or use and continue to drink or use until their heart was content (or they were so intoxicated they thought it was). Then they'd get up the next morning and do it all over again.

There's a term for someone who pretends, who lives their life this way: "functioning addict." I didn't know it at the time, but *I*, too, was pretending, and had been living like a functioning addict. (Just without the "addict" part.)

As the months dragged on after Joseph's death, my life had slowly found a new rhythm. As I have said, the first weeks were turbulent as I tried to navigate my grief. I struggled to process a life-shattering event in the midst of a flood of visitors; in time I grew lonely, bitter, and finally angry when those same people went back to their lives, leaving me alone with my thoughts. Persistent doubts led me to question my faith in God while experiencing the Great Sadness of realizing Joseph would never come back.

Without a doubt, this past year had been a ceaseless emotional roller coaster. One thing I came to realize, though, especially as my anger faded, was that many of those individuals who passed through my life, who offered help in some form and then moved on, weren't bad people after all. They didn't abandon me. Life had simply moved on for them. They had other obligations to attend to and their own lives to live. And I realized that, just as their lives had to return to normal, mine did too. Whatever "normal" meant.

This was when I made a decision to start functioning again.

The roller-coaster feeling lessened. In its place began a long, flat road that went on and on, day after day. *Did a giant hole still exist in my heart?* Of course. Did every day still feel like torture? Yes, very much so. My son was gone. But there was nothing I could do about this, and to be honest, I was emotionally exhausted. Finding some sort of solace in routine, in doing normal things, felt good. It was definitely better than picking up a bottle, or something worse.

At the end of each day of functioning—of hanging on—when I felt like I had done enough, I would go to bed and sleep away my pain. It sounds sad to say this but sleeping (or trying to, at least) became the best part of my life. At least I didn't have to feel anything when I wasn't awake. The problem was I could only sleep for about an hour and a half before reality would sneak back into my brain and jolt me awake with that awful, familiar suffering. Then the hole in my heart would ache, reminding me my son was dead. Hours would pass, morning would come, and I'd have to start "functioning" again.

Now that I was back among the living, I started running into people at the supermarket and passing them on the street, leading to many questions like "How you doing?" and "You eating?" and "You sleeping?" It also meant not exactly answering those questions, at least not honestly. No one *really* wants to hear how I wake up every morning at 1:30 a.m. with a stabbing pain in my chest or how I wonder if I will ever get through a day without bawling my eyes out.

One day I was talking to someone on the phone, and he asked, "How are you doing?" like everyone does. And I gave him my usual response, which was, "Oh, you know, I get by …" or something like that. But then, he asked again. He wanted to know how I *really* was. So much so, he actually waited for me to answer.

So, I told him exactly how I felt: "Like a functioning alcoholic."

This was the best way to describe the way I had been living—going through the motions every day, waiting for my nightly escape. And then, the craziest thing happened. Just by expressing aloud I had this problem, it went away—or at least I was able to start solving it. It was like they say in Alcoholics Anonymous: The first step is admitting you *have* a problem.

I had taken my first step.

I couldn't have done it without my friend on the phone. Even though I was in a dark place, it was one of the first moments I felt like someone actually cared enough to go in there with me. That's how his question hit me. It cut through all the darkness and went straight to my heart. It gave me permission to express what I was feeling. That was the beginning of my recovery.

Not long afterward, another friend called. "Have you been sleeping?" she asked.

I thought about my experience with my other friend, the fact he actually cared enough to hear the answer. So, I took a deep breath and said, "No."

"That's what I thought," my friend replied.

She told me she had been worried about me and encouraged me to see a professional. So, I called my doctor, who prescribed a sleeping pill allowing me four blissful hours of sleep every night. It wasn't eight hours, but it was something, and it helped with my commitment to "functioning." Again, all due to another friend who cared. Thankfully, when I woke up, I was no longer consumed with trying to escape my thoughts. Instead, I began searching for acceptance.

If I was going to move on with my life, I reasoned, I had to really, truly accept Joseph was gone. But as hard as I tried to get this through my brain, the moment of acceptance, of letting go, of whatever it was supposed to feel like (since I had no idea) never came. *Why not? Was I still not owning up to my grief? Was I still not coming from a real place? What more did I need to do?*

That's when, as I often do, I returned to my prayers and asked the Lord for answers. This is when the Lord told me I was the Great Pretender. Which, of course, sparked a deluge of more questions.

"Have I not been real? Have I not been honest in telling people how I feel? Am I hiding from them what this grief walk is really like? Am I not yet declaring the Truth of Your Word? How am I pretending, Lord?"

And the Lord answered, because He knows everything: "You seem to be what you're not, you see ... you're weary, but no one can tell."

That's when I understood what He meant by being the Great Pretender. Yes, I was back in the world, talking to others, and trying to be honest. But at the same time, I was still holding back, telling half the story, giving people *glimpses* but not presenting the full picture. Even though I was sharing my grief, I was still only revealing what I wanted others to know. I was only showing the parts I wanted them to see.

"Amid everything that I am bringing you through," the Lord said, "you are pretending that you're doing well. You're pretending that everything is okay. But if you hold back the depth of your pain, you will be holding back the depth of My deliverance."

This was certainly a new way to think about what I was going through. *Holding back in expressing my pain was somehow an affront to Him?* Then again, it made sense. It's like I was denying His awesome power.

Then God commanded me, "Stop covering up the wound. You will not heal completely if you keep hiding what really hurts. Reveal it. Be honest with yourself. Be honest with Me. Let others know you are not okay, but you can be. You shall be."

It became so clear. God was telling me to confront my pain in order to deal with it. And, as usual, He was right. Suffering is not pretty. Glossing over it does not help. It's like a bad coat of paint; it doesn't make anything look better, it doesn't hide imperfections, it just makes them shiny.

It was REAL TALK, and it came straight from the Lord.

Oh, yes, I'm the great pretender. Adrift in a world of my own. I've played the game, but to my real shame. You've left me to grieve all alone ...

So, I moved forward with a new commitment to be real in all things. Around this time, I learned Joseph's best friend Anthony had died. Unbelievably, it happened almost two years to the day after Joseph's passing. What a blow! It hit us almost as hard as it hit his family—after all, our boys grew up together, so they were like our family, too. Beyond this, there were so many uncanny parallels, it was like reliving the experience of Joseph's death. Especially the funeral.

The last time we had walked into that church was the day we buried our son. Now, we were back, and it was like nothing had changed. The warm, late summer day, the smell of fresh flowers, the somber faces of the mourners, the hugs and "I'm sorrys" and "Is there anything I can dos?" Even some of the words of the service were the same.

And so was the pain, unfortunately. I gasped and clutched my chest when I first glimpsed the white coffin with yet another young man's body inside. The sight took my breath away, forcing me to hold onto Jeff to steady myself as we entered into that sanctuary, just as we had for Joseph.

It was like living through hell all over again.

At Joseph's funeral, Anthony had told the story of how he and Joseph became best friends by riding their bikes together around in a circle for a week. Now, other friends shared stories of Anthony. Another candle snuffed out. Another young man gone too soon.

"These things should not be," I repeated to the Lord as I prayed for Anthony's family— just as I had for my own countless times before. A parent is not supposed to bury their child. I knew from personal experience. I *knew* this family's pain in every inch of my body.

When I woke the next morning, I discovered I had slipped back a little. I felt tired, overwhelmed, shaken. Weary. Once again overshadowed by grief. *Does the pain ever end, Lord? When will it go away?*

That's a question I haven't been able to answer yet. For a long time, I have struggled with Joseph's death. I still have my questions. I still have my doubts. In the midst of my joy, I still cry. I still sit awake some nights. I still want to hide in bed some days. Losing a child, grieving for a child, is like a never-ending nightmare.

The only solace comes when you sleep, but I like I said, when you awake you can't help remembering the nightmare is real. You're living it. Your child is gone. The worst thing that could possibly happen, the thing you believed could never happen, *would never happen*, happened. And yet you are still alive, still on Earth to face it and continue to live it, every single day God gives you.

Too real is this feeling
of make believe.
Too real when I feel
what my heart can't conceal.

I'm still fighting to overcome my grief on a daily basis, sometimes moment by moment. Every day I face the harsh reality: *This is how it is.* And so, I continue to push on. I pretend. I force the smile I'm expected to wear. I put on nice clothes to brighten my spirit. Wear my bow ties in honor of Joseph who loved them so much. Every way I can think of, I wear them: bow ties in my ears, on my fingers, on my neck, on my nails, on my wrists, on my wallet and even my pocketbook. Likewise, I do the things that make me happy—or used to, anyway. I go shopping and do puzzles. I play those silly little Facebook games. And all the while this thing called grief still gnaws at me.

Yes, I'm the great pretender.
(Just like the Lord said).
Just laughin' and gay like a clown.
I seem to be what I'm not, you see.
I'm wearing my heart like a crown.
Pretending that you're still around.

I know I'm not pretending Joseph is still around. But Anthony's death stirred the pot yet again, brought those raw emotions from when we first lost our son back to the surface. Which means, yet again, I have to make an adjustment. This is what living with grief feels like—a series of adjustments, all to make the pain as bearable as possible. But future adjustments would now be made with one exception: I was done pretending. I was over trying to be someone I was not. No more meaningless platitudes or cliché church sayings coming out of my mouth.

And that's still true today. I knew I couldn't heal from my son's death by following the rules of society, worrying about Who says What, or Where or How Things Must Be Done. I just couldn't do it by being politically correct. I won't ever pretend any more. I can't pretend any more. I can only survive this by being me, and I can only do that by revealing my pain. The pain of the gut-wrenching-honest, take-your-breath-away truth about death. About grief.

As I do, then as God did for me—with the comfort He has given me—I may be able to bring some comfort to others. Without reservation, without pretense.

No more great pretending for me.

Chapter 10: Acceptance

Acceptance: The action of consenting to receive or undertake something offered.

The other day, I saw Joseph driving. My brain struggled to process what it was seeing as I watched my son behind the wheel of his 2005 Honda Civic.

Joseph's favorite car was a Camaro. He dreamed of buying one and was saving his money for it. That was his plan. His dad was going to help him. He used to see Camaros all the time and text me pictures of them, telling me, "Look what parked next to me. I'm telling you, I'm getting one, Mom."

Christmas 2012, I found a Mattel Camaro and wrapped it up. We gave it to Joseph as a gift, and told him, "Hold on to it, the real one is coming." He didn't find it too funny. A moment later, my husband had him take something to the garage.

When Joseph entered, Jeff opened the garage door. There in the driveway was Joseph's new car with a bow on top. He was so excited! We gave him the key and he got right in it, taking Christian in with him. They just sat in the driveway checking out the car. It wasn't much, but it was a safe car. We wanted to make sure his first car was a practical one (how about that?). It wasn't a Camaro, but he appreciated it just the same. *It was his.*

And now here I was seeing Joseph in that car, making his way to work, taking the jug-handle turn the road required. I felt an ominous feeling in the pit of my stomach. Joseph was a safe driver. He always gave everybody ratings about how they drove, and decided he was the second-safest driver in the house (his dad was first). Joe loved his dad so much.

But I knew in my heart that didn't matter in this moment. It started to pound as he rounded the corner and made his way into the intersection, looking straight ahead at the road in front of him.

Don't do it, I thought. *Please, Joseph, don't do it.*

Then I saw it. The car speeding down the road toward the intersection. The light was red, but the car was going so fast, I knew it wouldn't stop. I knew it was going to plow right through the intersection into my unknowing son.

How was I seeing this? Where was I? I felt like I was standing somewhere off just to the side where no one could detect me, like I wasn't quite connected to the scene. I was observing it, but not *in* it. I tried desperately to connect with reality and with my son. I screamed out to Joseph to look, to get out of the way, to *hurry*. But no sound came out of my mouth.

Instead, I heard the deafening sound of the crash.

As the speeding car hit Joseph, he swerved, doing almost a complete 180 to face the opposite direction before coming to a stop. And I saw Joseph, or what I guessed was Joseph's spirit, step out of the car. I watched as he looked down at his lifeless body in the crumpled wreck.

Strangely, there was no emotion. For a split second, it was as if he was just observing.

Then, suddenly, I jolted awake. Just another nightmare.

I changed my position, sitting straight up in bed, trying to clear my head, to stop reliving the horrible moment yet again. How many times over the past year had I struggled to make the pain, the nightmares, and the sadness stop?

Nothing worked. The pain never ceased because Joseph never returned.

I also was haunted by these recurring questions: Did Joseph feel anything when the car hit him? Did he see it coming and experience the terror of knowing what was about to happen? Did he feel his bones shatter at the moment of impact? Or did it all happen so fast he never felt anything at all? I played this scene over in my mind obsessively. What, exactly, did Joseph experience? To get away from such terrible questions, I had to force my brain to concentrate on other things.

Huckily, God knows our thoughts, our every concern. His Word says He will perfect those things that matter to us. He will give us peace beyond understanding. So later, when I prayed, I told Him about my dream and God had an answer. He told me he sent the dream to me specifically to quiet my fears. He showed me Joseph didn't feel the impact by letting me see my son's spirit leaving his body.

"I protected him," He reassured me.

Still, it's a funny thing to wrap your head around. How could He have protected Joseph when I saw Joseph with my own eyes, all beat up and bruised in that hospital bed with tubes and wires everywhere? Yet God still protected him. He protected Joseph's spirit.

Though my son's body was broken, his spirit remained intact. And his spirit felt no pain.

God also told me He did not allow Joseph to see the car coming toward him, so he did not experience fear before the impact. That meant my son's last moments of consciousness on Earth were free from pain and fear. And this understanding meant everything to me. My body flooded with relief and all the tension poured out of me.

I really do believe the Lord protected Joseph in those horrific moments. So that morning, I recounted the dream to God during my devotional. And as I began to journal about it, I realized I wasn't just sitting up. I was also breathing. Again.

~~~

I spent the first year of my grief journey after I lost Joseph waiting. What was I waiting for? I didn't exactly know. The moment when it would all be okay? A point of clarity when I would finally understand why my son was taken? I wasn't sure. I only knew I was waiting for a moment when life would feel normal again—for a thing I called "acceptance."

But the moment never came.

Instead, I kept experiencing and re-experiencing the same grief stages. I went back and forth from anger, to disbelief, to shock, to sadness, to loneliness, and finally, to functionality again. Then, just when I felt like I was doing okay and life was moving along, I'd be overwhelmed by the pain, or the sadness, or the anger, and the whole horrible cycle would start over.

But one day, something changed.

I realized (or God allowed me to see) what acceptance really meant. It didn't mean losing Joseph would *ever* be okay, or his death would ever stop hurting, or I would ever "move on" from his loss. It meant it was time for me to accept the reality of where I was in life and stop waiting for some magical moment when things would go back to "normal"—to the way they were before Joseph died.

The person I used to be was buried the day I lost my son. And she wasn't coming back any sooner than he was. Life as I knew it had forever changed, and it would never go back to the same. All I could do was move forward. It was the only option.

To accomplish this, I had to accept what had happened to Joseph. That he was not "chosen" to die, but simply, because we live in an imperfect world, one man made a decision to run a red light, and as a result, my son lost his life. Heartbreaking as it was, Joseph was dead. This was, is, and always will be my reality, and there is nothing I could have done or can do to change it.

So, it's okay if I still feel angry, or bitter, or sad sometimes. Because, at other times, I feel acceptance. That's how grief works, at least for me. It's an ever-changing journey, evolving along with me as I walk my path.

As an almost-official "grief expert," I can tell you this does not mean there is a "right way" to grieve. There's no single path or set progression of steps for graduating to the "next level." And there's certainly no point when you're "done." Grief is a never-ending process of learning to live with loss, and it includes a range of emotions that can change from day to day, or even moment to moment. Just know, if you are grieving, there will come a point when you will stop waiting for what comes next, and instead accept your life as it is—pain and all.

You'll stop waiting for what's next and start dealing with what *is*. Today, there are times during my grief walk when I can move past simply functioning to this kind of acceptance. I'm not pardoning what happened to my son or condoning it or saying everything is right with my world. I'm accepting everything is *not* going to be right in my world. And that's okay.

So, I accept that a tragedy has been brought into my family's lives and our loved one has been taken away. I accept he is no longer here with us on Earth, and this is the way it will be, as hard a pill as it is to swallow. I've been overwhelmed with sadness at many points over the course of this journey—so many I lose count. Sometimes the sadness is enough to bring me to my knees. But I understand now this is part of the grieving process, just like those days when I'm angry at the world, when I can't believe what has happened to my family, when I don't feel like getting out of bed at all.

But there are also days when I accept my life as it is now, when I know I must still be here for a reason. I accept the Lord wants me to go on. So, I do.

~~~

Very often, we must endure suffering and hardship in order to grow. Growth requires alone time and separation in a place, a remote or desolate place, we may think of as the "wilderness." Immediately after John baptized Jesus and God declared "This is My beloved Son," the Bible says in Matthew 4:1, "Then Jesus was led by the Spirit into the wilderness to be tempted by the devil."

Some people come to the conclusion, just as Job's friends did, that when a person struggles through their time in the wilderness, it's because God is punishing them. "They must have done something wrong," they assume, "to be forced to endure so much suffering." Or, as many have said, they are simply "reaping what they have sown."

Not so.

Go back and read Scripture again. It says the Spirit *led* Jesus into the wilderness. The Spirit of God directed Him there. The Spirit of God ordered His very steps right into suffering. And suffer He did. He spent 40 days and 40 nights in the wilderness, fasting in agony. Of course, the devil showed up during this time. To tempt Jesus. To make His suffering even greater. Three times, the enemy tormented the Lord with something He might have desperately wanted. But Jesus knew those temptations were not what He *needed.*

The enemy does the same thing to us regular mortals, too. Troubling us, plaguing us, torturing us with thoughts and desires we would never even consider if we were not alone and suffering in some way. But if God leads you into the wilderness, know He has a purpose behind it. He has a reason for doing so. And we do God an injustice when we believe otherwise.

I, myself, am guilty of this. Most of us are. We're only human, after all. We humans also sometimes fail to understand God's purpose in leading us into the wilderness in the first place—as if, somehow, He is calling us to rest, and since He led us there, He won't let anything trouble us. Again, not true. Remember, the attacks did not begin until *after* the Spirit of God led Jesus into the wilderness. For some of us, those attacks still come.

God separates us. He calls us apart. He brings us onto the mountaintop for a time and He brings us into the wilderness for a time. Those are periods of testing. Periods of refreshing. Times to grow and stretch our faith.

But during those times, which can often be trying, we are not and will not be immune from attacks by the enemy. His whole purpose is to kill, steal and destroy no matter who you are, where you are, and regardless of whether or not God brought you there.

It's important to know that even when you are fasting and praying, you will not necessarily be protected from temptation. But you must go on. And even when the worst happens, when you are tested the most, when you are pushed to your breaking point, whose strength will you lean on? You can rely on your own strength and pray with everything you've got. But you will fall, every single time. Because you can't do it without God.

In God's strength, and in the power of His Word, you will be able to stand. In God's strength, you will be refreshed through your wilderness journey. And, at the very moment when you need it most, you will be given sufficient grace to get through it.

God certainly has a plan for us. The Word says it's a good plan, a plan for you to prosper, to not to suffer needless harm, to give you hope and direct you toward your future. Just as He did with Jesus.

Thanks be unto God for He is real. Even in the wilderness.

~~~

My journey through grief and toward acceptance reminded me of this concept of the wilderness. After all, the wilderness is a place of trials and hardship. It is a place where your faith will be tested, where you will be forced to declare what you believe. But it is also a place where God dwells, to lead you, to guide you, to correct you, to prove His Word to you.

While the wilderness is a place of pain, this suffering does not lack purpose. And once you accept the reality that you are, in fact, *in* the wilderness, and you accept what has happened to bring you there, you can begin to heal and to move on. You can begin to grow past your pain, into whoever God intends for you to become.

It took me a long time to truly accept Joseph was gone—that I will only see him in visions and dreams, until one day, I will see him in heaven. I know that until that day, he will be gone from my life. And it hurts. Still. Badly.

But part of acceptance is living through the pain and enduring it, without trying to run away from it or pretend it isn't there. It's accepting what has happened and living with and processing and enduring through the pain to reach the next step, or the next chapter the Author and the Finisher of your faith has written.

When we get to the point at which we can accept what has happened, we finally get to the point of forgiveness. And, more importantly, we can find peace.

Chapter 11: Forgiveness

Forgiveness: The action or process of forgiving or being forgiven. The act or process of letting go of an offense

It was a day I thought I'd never see. We were sitting in a courtroom, just a few feet away from Raymond Blinn—the man who killed my son—waiting for the outcome of the wrongful death lawsuit against him. We had brought the case after the state declined to press criminal charges against Blinn, despite determining he had knowingly "disregarded" a red light and run it anyway. We didn't care about the money and we didn't expect an apology. But we were determined to receive justice.

Now, more than 2½ years since Joseph was taken from us, would justice finally come?

I held my breath as I waited to finally, hopefully, hear Raymond Blinn held responsible for killing my son. As I have repeatedly said, I was very angry at Blinn. I thought about him often, trying to wrap my mind around how wrong it was that a then-74-year-old man could run a red light, cause an accident stealing the life of a 22-year-old, then just walk away.

Blinn had lived his life. My son's whole life was ahead of him. There was simply no universe in which what happened to my Joe was right or fair.

And then, for the state to decline to charge Raymond Blinn? To issue a couple of traffic citations and allow him to simply go on as before—after he took a human life? It was just unfathomable.

However, deep down inside, I knew that one day I would have to forgive Raymond Blinn. Regardless of what he had done to my child, I would have to find a way to move forward. If only to go on with my own life, not to mention be right with the Lord, I had to forgive this man.

I just had no idea how that was ever going to happen.

But now, here we were, back in our Sunday best again, this time in a courtroom. Just Jeff, my daughter Brandi and me. (As much as we wanted Jasmine with us, she was working on a case in Chicago that she could not step away from.) Of course, our attorneys were present, as well as a few family friends—

yet another painful reminder for me of just how small our circle had become. We sat in the front row waiting for justice. Meanwhile, on the other side of the aisle, Raymond Blinn, his wife Patricia, his attorneys, and the insurance company adjuster also sat in silence, awaiting the outcome.

You know the expression, "You could hear a pin drop"? That's how quiet it was in that courtroom. I think I was afraid to breathe.

At last, the judge picked up a piece of paper and began to read the words that would determine the fate of Raymond Blinn—and in some ways, the fate of my family. The resolution read something like this: "It has been determined by the State of New Jersey, County of Burlington, that in the case of Evelyn and Jeffery Fannell, on behalf of the Estate of Joseph M. Fannell, as the plaintiff vs. Raymond Blinn, the defendant Raymond Blinn is responsible for the wrongful death of Joseph Fannell."

Responsible for the wrongful death of Joseph Fannell ...

Shock tore through me. I couldn't believe it. What else did I feel? It wasn't exactly joy, since the verdict would not bring Joseph back. Neither would it erase the pain of the past 2½ years, or of the years and decades without Joseph stretching ahead of us.

Still … it felt … different. Turning to Jeff and Brandi I noticed they looked just as stunned. Before we could even respond to each other, Blinn's attorneys were right there beside us, shaking our hands, saying "Congratulations."

"*Congratulations?*" I couldn't help thinking. "For what?"

I also couldn't help noticing Jeff did not shake their hands.

Then, the most remarkable, perhaps unbelievable, thing of all happened. Patricia Blinn approached me, arms extended. I looked around in panic, not knowing what to do. *What can you do when the wife of your son's killer wants to hug you? What's appropriate? Should I curse her? Ignore her? Something worse?*

Still grappling with this dilemma, I noticed Brandi looking at me, wondering how I would respond, her eyes filling with tears. Then I saw Jeff. I saw everyone, really. Our attorneys, our friends, all staring back at me, wondering what I would do next.

Suddenly all I could do was reach out, first with one arm, then the other. I hugged her, I hugged Patricia, the wife of the man who killed my son.

That's when the tears came.

"I'm so sorry," she said, tears pouring down her face too. "I'm a mother and a grandmother. I have a grandson who is about the same age your son would be now. I cannot even imagine..." Her voice broke.

Lord, it had happened.

Not only did I receive an apology, a sincere expression of remorse, but I saw firsthand grace and mercy, love and forgiveness. I felt *God*. Not only in Patricia, but in myself. The thing we "people of faith" talk about often, but practice so much less.

The burden lifted off of my heart as I finally, finally felt forgiveness.

The ice broke at that moment as around me everyone was crying and hugging. Jeff threw his arms around me. Together we embraced Brandi. The three of us wound up standing there in a sort of semi-circle, crying and hugging. Then others joined us. Our friends walked up to our little cluster and hugged each one of us, one by one. Even our lawyers hugged us while motioning for us to leave the courtroom. We did, still holding on to each other the entire way.

We found our way downstairs where a man was waiting for us. The first witness at the accident scene, he told us how he found Joseph, how he picked my son up after it happened and held him in his arms. I started to cry, and so did he. Soon everyone was crying again as Jeff held onto me and the witness described what had occurred that horrible morning years ago.

Then his wife came over and hugged us. "We are so sorry for your loss," she said. "We have children too."

It made me feel a little better knowing someone had been with Joseph and actually held him. I hugged Jeff again and we held on to each other until we left the courthouse.

~ ~ ~

As I type this story, I realize we were blessed that day. Not everyone has the benefit of so many loved ones comforting them. Not everyone gets the benefit of a big, movie-moment scene of justice. Not everyone receives a judge who says, "You are right, and they are wrong" and actually makes someone pay for what they've done. Not everyone gets congratulations and apologies and hugs. After all of that time begging God for some kind of closure, through His grace I was given more than I ever dared to dream.

Before Joseph died, in my past life—before I knew the need for forgiveness—I wrote a blog post about it. It turns out there was some wisdom there even though I had no clue what was in store for me:

We have to understand forgiveness is not something that mostly benefits the other person, it benefits us more than we know. Unforgiveness hurts you. If you refuse to forgive someone, they may hurt momentarily, but you are the one hurt in the end, and even more so. Because God requires YOU to forgive. He doesn't ask you. He is not trying to coax you. He is not comforting you. In most cases, God is not even HEARING you.

The Word says in Matthew 6:14-15, "For if you forgive other people when they sin against you, your heavenly Father will also forgive you. But if you DO NOT forgive others their sins, your Father WILL NOT forgive your sins."

In the Lord's Prayer Jesus said the way we ought to pray is this, "And forgive us our debts, as we also forgive our debtors." (Matthew 6:12). Then in Colossians 3:12-13 it says "as God's chosen people, holy and dearly loved, clothe yourselves with compassion, kindness, humility, gentleness and patience. Bear with each other and forgive one another if any of you has a grievance against someone. Forgive as the Lord forgave you." Continuing in Ephesians it says, "Get rid of all bitterness, rage, anger, harsh words, and slander, as well as all types of evil behavior. Instead, be kind to each other, tenderhearted, forgiving one another, just as God through Christ has forgiven you" (v. 31-32 NLT).

Sounds like we don't have a choice in the matter. We are to forgive as the Lord forgives us ... and God doesn't wait to forgive us. It's instant. As many times as we break His heart, He forgives us. He is not waiting until we are ready to be forgiven. He is not waiting until HE is ready to forgive us. This is our example, and this is what we must follow. Ready or not.

In the parable of the unforgiving servant (Matthew 18:21-35) Peter asks how many times must we forgive? And Jesus says, 70 times 7, which is at least 490 times. So, unless you have forgiven someone 490 times, you still need to forgive. Jesus then goes on to tell the story about the servant who begged to be forgiven of his debts and was forgiven by his master. But then the servant had someone under him ask him for forgiveness, and the servant refused to forgive him. When the master returned to find this situation, the servant was tortured until he forgave. At the end of the Scripture text, Jesus says "This is how my heavenly Father will treat each of you unless you forgive your brother or sister from your heart."

This is us. We are the servants. God is the Master. We constantly not only ask Him to forgive us but expect Him to forgive us and He does. But when we as the servant have been wronged by others, we want to throw them in the dungeon and make them pay endlessly for what they have done. These things should not be. God forgives you. You need to forgive others.

God shared two things with me recently. First, I was told, "Forgiveness is accepting an apology that was not given." Second, He let me know, "Forgiveness is being able to apologize for something you did not do."

So, if I have stepped on your toes today, forgive me. If I have already done something to you and you forgave me for that, forgive me again. For your Father in heaven says, "Forgive and you shall be forgiven. If you do not forgive, neither will I forgive you."

~~~

After Joseph died, I learned just how much God asks when he commands us to forgive. For three years, the same woman who so confidently wrote the blog post you just read could not conceive of forgiving Raymond Blinn for what he had done.

If anything, I was furious at the man. He never apologized for running that red light and taking my son from me, not once. He never expressed how sorry he was, never sent condolences, never said one word. And, in my anger, I became fixated on the need to hear those words from his mouth. As if this would somehow make it all okay. As if this would somehow bring Joseph back.

But in the courtroom, when the wife of my son's killer reached out and hugged me, I was reminded of so much. Her outstretched arms brought me back to God's mercy, her actions showed me how in spite of what we do, He always extends His arms (both of them) to hug us. And in that moment, I no longer needed the apology. It no longer mattered.

God told me why it happened. Why I finally received the thing I had been obsessing over and demanding and begging for and just generally *needing* for almost three years. *"Forgiveness is accepting an apology that was not given."* The moment I let go of needing to hear those words, once I stretched my own arms back toward Patricia Blinn and wrapped them around her, I received it—at long last when I realized Raymond Blinn didn't matter anymore. This is when God showed me that true forgiveness is receiving an apology you will never get. When I finally could truly feel,

"I don't care about the apology," that's when it came.

My moment with Patricia reminded me of something I often say to others: "Women are special in the eyes of God." I tell it to the women in my church, I mention it to the women at the Annual Tea Social our church hosts, I say it so much because I truly believe we are special. We have His heart. God said it was because of Abigail, the wife of Nabal, that David did not kill him. She asked for mercy on behalf of her husband and because of that, her husband was spared.

God said it was because of Patricia Blinn, how she reached out to embrace me with open arms, that her husband received the grace he had been given. Because of his wife's actions, the husband received forgiveness.

And it was because of God that I was able to extend it. Only God.

Not that it hasn't been a painful, humbling, and at times exhausting journey. Because there's really nothing God can do for me *until* I recognize the limit of what I can do for myself as a human being. Only then, when I am on my knees, is He allowed to do the impossible: forgiving, letting go, extending grace to the man who killed my son.

He is forgiven, because I am. And because I am forgiven, I am free. Justice (for me) has been served. And I believe this is what Joseph would want for any one of us.

Sleep in peace, my Joe.

Chapter 12: Peace

Peace: Freedom from disturbance; quiet and tranquility; the concept of harmony and the absence of hostility; a pact or agreement to end hostilities between those who have been at war or in a state of enmity.

It was a warm Saturday afternoon. I was in the kitchen making dinner, and Christian was at the house, shooting hoops in the driveway like he always does when he comes over. As usual, I went back and forth between the kitchen and the garage, watching him shoot hoops, just as I did with Joseph. I listened to the familiar THUMP-THUMP-THUMP *swish* of the ball as it smacked against the pavement, then sailed up through the air and into the net. I smiled to myself. A perfect three. Just like his Uncle Joe taught him ...

Oh. Joseph ...

My hand went to my heart as I felt the familiar sharp pain, then the dull, empty ache that always followed. Just like it did, and still does, every time I remember something about my child. Something that happens roughly 700 times a day.

Then, as I made my way back towards the kitchen, I caught a glimpse of Jeff, who had wandered into the kitchen for something to drink. He was standing by the refrigerator, listening to the basketball THUMP-THUMP-THUMP *swishing* through the net again.

He must have felt me watching him because he turned and met my gaze. His eyes were a mirror of what he probably saw in mine. Sadness. Pain. Loss. Understanding. And ultimately, love. In that moment, without saying a word, we spoke volumes. Then he opened the refrigerator and took out one of his energy drinks, and I went back to peeling potatoes.

Because life goes on.

For 39 years (36 of them married), Jeff and I have been a team. Since we were 17 years old. We've been through everything together—financial issues, sick kids, you name it—and weathered some major storms. But Joseph's death threw us off our marriage game in a way nothing else could. For a long time, we walked around in our own individual bubbles of pain, not wanting to say or do anything that might trigger a memory in the other or might cause them suffering. We were both thinking of

Joseph, feeling Joseph, missing and grieving Joseph. But we mostly did it alone.

Losing a child is hard on a marriage because it changes you. It's like losing a part of yourself—like an arm or a leg, only deeper. You know that part of you that can feel pure joy in every inch of your body and soul, from the top of your head to the tip of your toes? That's what you lose. You're a different person. A less joyful person. Definitely not the same person you were when you got married. And your spouse is a different person, too.

So somehow, in dealing with our grief, Jeff and I lost each other a little. We lost the bond we once had when we faced every single other thing that came our way through the years. It had always been us against the world. Me and him. Him and me. But after Joseph's death, there was no longer an *us*. Grief took that away. It caused us to lose sight of who we were, as individuals and as a team. Instead, we suffered alone. Until one day, when we looked at each other and said, "We need to get *us* back."

It's a funny thing … ironically funny. In the fall of 2014, I was going through some personal issues that brought me to a therapist. I believe the Lord also led me to do so, because in dealing with some of my personal issues, this therapist also helped me deal with some of my past, and yes, even with what was to come. So, when Jeff and I started to lose each other, I immediately thought we should go and see her.

At first, I went alone. Then, we went together. During our session, I talked a lot about Joe and about how difficult coping with his death had been, and it helped. Then Jeff went for a solo visit and immediately realized therapy wasn't for him. As a man of God, he knew he had to rely on God to help him to heal his broken heart, so he could help me with mine.

And God did. God was. God is. Still helping him and healing him. And before long, I realized I no longer needed therapy, only trust in God. Jeff and I decided we would just love each other through the pain. And we did.

And we do.

~ ~ ~

Nothing else matters
than seeing You, Jesus.
Seeking the Master,
the One who reigns over my life.

Nothing else matters
than seeing You, Jesus.
Just to sit at Your feet,
hear Your voice clearly speak,
lifts me out of defeat,

for in You I'm complete;
it reminds me that nothing else,
nothing else matters.
Nothing Else Matters
~by Marvin Sapp

When Whitney Houston died a few years before Joseph's passing, I was devastated. I spent days praying for her daughter and her family, asking, "Why, Lord? She was making a comeback." I was sure she was finally ready to return from whatever had pulled her away from her God-given talent. Why did she have to die and leave so many people heartbroken? It just didn't make sense.

One day while I was praying, the Lord, as he often does, answered me. "Because I loved her more," he said.

His words struck me as strange. Still, I said, "Of course, you do, Lord. No one could love anyone more than you do."

Later, I brought it up to my daughter Brandi, and her response was: "Yeah, but God is *always* going to love someone more than we can. He's
God."

It didn't exactly explain why Whitney had to die. But time passed, and
eventually I sort of lost track of the whole thing.

Fast forward a couple of months. Our friend and Pastor Kenneth Hackett sent us a song along with instructions to listen to it *three times*. The song was *Nothing Else Matters*. I did as he requested and played it aloud in the house three times. However, I liked it so much I let it play again and again, over and over, quietly in the background as I went about my chores throughout the morning.

In other words, I didn't exactly follow Pastor Hackett's instructions. I did not stop after three listens. Isn't that the way it goes sometimes when someone gives us instructions? We take them lightly. We expand them or reduce them based on what we want or on our own ideas about of what we're doing. We forget there is a reason God warns us against leaning unto our own understanding. We forget our understanding has limits.

We do it with recipes. We'll replace this ingredient with that one because we like it better or we're out of something and this other thing is probably just as good, right? Or maybe we shorten or lengthen the cooking time or change the oven temperature because we're in a hurry or we think we know better. Then we wonder why whatever we made doesn't taste right. We do it with instructions on how to repair something. We skip a part or don't do the steps in order or take a shortcut, and then we wonder why the fix doesn't hold.

And we even do it with a person of God (in my case, Pastor Hackett) who God places in our lives to give us the instructions in the first place! We fail to do what they say, which can't be good. Just think about what might have happened if the woman did not fully obey what Elijah had told her...

God instructs us to take heed of full instruction and sometimes we fall short. We may even take heed, but we find a way to change it up. We take away from it or we add to it, which is what I did when I listened to that song over and over instead of stopping after three times. But thank God for grace. Always working things out for the good. Even when we don't follow His instructions.

Anyway, a few days after I listened to the song, I received an article in the mail about heaven. The author wrote about two people, a man and a woman, each of whom had suffered a near-death situation. And while the man went on to be with the Lord, the woman chose to stay on Earth.

That's right. *Chose* to stay.

The author explained she had a specific reason for using the word "chose." She believed the woman was not "ready" to die.

But who can be ready to die? Who *will* be ready to die?

I believe Joseph was ready to die.

Did I lose you there?

I'll say it again. I believe Joseph was ready to die. My dear son, whom I loved since the day he was born. Who did not cause the accident, did not choose it, did not even conceive of it...was ready to die.

I know this probably sounds crazy. But stay with me. I promise this will all come together in the end.

In the article I received in the mail, the author said when the man who died was in the presence of God, he was presented with a choice: He could either remain on this Earth or enter heaven. The author believed in that moment, the man felt the love of God so strongly he chose to go. He *had* to go.

So, what does this have to do with Whitney Houston and my Joe? Let's start with Whitney. I'm no celebrity expert, but from what I've heard about Whitney Houston— from the media and the friends and associates who spoke about her in the days following her death—one thing was clear. The woman was in pain. Despite her success, her talent, the fact that she was rich and famous and beloved by so many people, she was suffering. The love of man wasn't enough to stop her pain.

When God told me, "I loved her more," I didn't get it. Now, all these years later, I think I understand what He meant. As much as Whitney was loved by her daughter, her mother, her family, her friends and her fans, their love was imperfect. It was not enough to make up for whatever was missing in her life, and it could not erase the pain she was clearly experiencing on this Earth. Her problems with drugs, her marital struggles with Bobby Brown, and more than anything, the pressure of having to be Whitney Houston, superstar, every single day, were too much. No matter how much she was loved by others, nothing could heal her pain.

But when she experienced the presence of God, she felt a love unlike anything her family and friends and millions of fans could provide. It was overpowering. Unconditional. It was healing. So, she opened her arms and God's love wrapped her up and He took her.

Which brings me to my son.

As I thought about my Joe, I remembered Whitney and how God had told me he loved her more than all of us here on Earth. I also remembered the words God wanted me to hear, us to hear, that He sent to me through Pastor Hackett a few weeks after Joseph died. NOTHING ELSE MATTERS. *"Nothing else matters than seeing You, Jesus."* And I realized it was a testimony from Joseph himself.

Nothing else mattered to my son except being with God. The love of God compelled him to go, welcoming him with open arms. And because God's love was so strong, so much stronger than the love he felt here on Earth, Joseph said, "Yes, Lord. I'll go with you."

Suddenly, it all made sense.

When God told my husband "I got your son," He *really* had my son. Joseph was in His presence, even before he was hit. That's why, when Joseph crossed into the intersection, I don't believe he saw the car coming. God protected him from that pain. If he had known, he would have moved. Somehow.

The Scripture says to be absent from the body is to be present with the Lord. I mentioned earlier how I used to obsess over whether or not Joseph felt pain when he was hit. Now, when I look back, I have to admit to myself, even though God protected him from seeing that car, that he *was* in pain. It just wasn't the kind of pain I had been worried about. Joseph did not feel pain from the accident. He felt pain from the state he was in and the monumental decision he had to make. *Should he stay or should he go?*

When I held my son's hand in the hospital that terrible day, even though he was in a semi-conscious state, I saw a tear fall from his eye. Now I believe I know why. He knew how much I loved him. He knew how much we all loved him—his father, his sisters, his family, his nephew. And he also knew God loved him more. Which meant he was facing a choice.

Being there in the presence of God, feeling His perfect love, Joseph knew he had to leave his life on Earth. His tear was his way of telling me he had to go, he had *chosen* to go. God asked and he said "yes," because the love of God compelled him to say yes. God loved him more than I could. More than any of us could.

In this moment of realization, I finally received peace.

I admit, it's an uneasy peace. As a mother, I don't like the idea that I loved Joe imperfectly. I loved him with everything I had and always will. But I'm still an imperfect human being, so my love was also imperfect. I don't like the idea that Joe experienced pain on this Earth. But we, his family, loved him with all our hearts, and we tried to help him, but we couldn't love him past his pain.

I don't like the idea that he chose to go, leaving us for a more perfect love, even knowing we are still here, left to mourn him forever. But I know what I saw in that hospital room. I know what I believe. I saw that tear drop from my youngest child's eye that day, no matter what the nurse called it or said caused it. I believe Joseph cried because he was hurting in his spirit for what his life was, and in his heart. Because as much as he knew we loved him, and as much as he loved us, he had to leave us. So, he shed one final tear for us.

It was his way of saying goodbye.

I will miss my son every day until I see him again in heaven. Until then, I know he is with the Lord, and I know the Lord loves him more than I ever could. And so, as much as my heart still hurts—I am at peace.

Because Joseph is at peace.

Psalm 34:18 says, "If your heart is broken, you'll find God right there; if you're kicked in the gut, he'll help you catch your breath."

Remember to breathe.

Afterword

We were headed down the highway toward Virginia, cruising along at 65 miles per hour, moving with the flow of traffic, no obstacles in our way. Then, all of a sudden, brake lights. Up ahead, stretching forward as far as we could see, was an enormous traffic jam. We slowed to almost a complete stop, trapped in what looked like a sea of cars, all going nowhere. It felt like we would never, ever get out.

But eventually, ever-so-slowly, the cars started inching forward. We began to move, just a few feet at a time at first, then a few more, a little faster than before. Then finally, the road opened up, the cars started traveling at normal speed and we broke free, driving straight ahead towards our destination.

We took this trip to visit friends just two months after we lost Joseph—so any similarity to my life at the time was probably lost on me. But looking back, that traffic jam feels like a fitting metaphor for what I've experienced in the months and years since the moment I lost my son.

Before Joseph's death, I was cruising along on the "highway of life." There were no major speed bumps in my way, I wasn't trying to move too fast or too slow or pass anybody to get ahead, I was staying in my lane, going with the flow, adjusting to road conditions as they happened.

In other words, I was living my life …

Until a man in a speeding car ran a red light and everything came to a standstill.

For a long time, that's where I stayed. At a standstill. But eventually, I started moving forward, little by little. After a while, the "highway" somehow opened up, and I began to move a little faster, and then faster still. And after some more time, the deep cloud of despair and sorrow evaporated, the road ahead cleared, and I was able to move forward.

In my experience, that's how the grieving process works. There were so many moments when I felt like I was locked in one place and no matter how hard I tried to move past my sorrow toward living a "normal life," I couldn't do it. I didn't realize, even when it felt like I was standing still, that I was actually making progress. It was just happening in such tiny increments, I didn't notice.

Healing from something as traumatic as the loss of a child is a long, painful process because it takes time to learn to live with the new reality of life without someone you love. It can't be about "getting back" to your old life or the person you used to be because you can't ever live that life or be that person again. All you can do is grow through the pain into a new version of yourself.

But you will—and that version can be better and stronger, albeit sadder, yes, than the person you were before. And when you're ready, the road ahead will open up, and you will be able to move forward and live your life.

I know, because it happened to me. Just like the road opened up for us on the way to Virginia, the road of my life opened up and allowed me to move forward and continue my life's journey.

Beyond the traffic jam, there's not much I remember about the trip to Virginia except, at some point, we arrived at our destination as planned. Just as I trust we will all get to our destination in life. We will continue to be whom God has called us to be, continue to do what He has called us to do, to complete our mission in life and get to our final destination.

I know my family and I will get there. And when we do, it will be glorious, because at last we will see our Savior and God along with our beloved Joseph. We will see our Joe again. We will get there. Until that day, we will continue to move forward.

Yes, even when it feels like we're only inching ahead, we will keep going.

I'll leave you with one final thought. When life throws you a curve, even if you hurt so much you feel like giving up or giving in, remember to breathe. Deeply. Hold on to that breath as though it were your last, and it will get you through the next moment. And you'll get through the next one, and the one after that, and the one after that...until that day when you see your beloved again.

Just remember to breathe.

Remember to Breathe

If I told you how I could get you through this
Would you find it hard to believe?
When tears like waves break through painful silence
And you fall down to your knees

Just remember to breathe,
remember to breathe
You have what you need inside
and you are still alive
So, remember to breathe

When the truth you believe
leaves you wounded and shaken,
And it causes you to retreat
When the wind you depended on
is suddenly taken
And the blow that was thrown
hurts so deep

Just remember to breathe,
remember to breathe
You have what you need inside,
and you are still alive
So remember to breathe

For every moment is a gift
And every precious day that you're here
Don't forget to breathe deeply

With every breath that you take
Know it's never too late
for God will make a way
And with one simple kiss,
your spirit will live again

If I told you now that the night
is almost over
And the sun will shine upon your face
Would you promise me
that you will dance before the Father?
Because there's so much to life
you must embrace
So, remember to breathe,
remember to breathe
You have what you need inside
Yes, you are yet alive, so remember to
breathe

For every moment is a gift
And every precious day you're here
Don't forget to breathe, breathe deeply

~Lyrics by Marcus Cole

About the Author

 Evelyn Fannell has the true heart of a servant. She spends a great deal of her time assisting friends, family, and others with a variety of plans and projects, always seeking simply to be of help; always going the extra mile. A writer since her youth, in 2008 Evelyn created the blog, *But God Is Real*, inspired by real life situations and circumstances that speak to the "realness" of God and His intervention in daily life. After the death of her son, Joseph, Evelyn started another blog, *In the Shadow of Grief,* created to chronicle the emotions and stages of grief so that she could help others through their journey of pain and sorrow. Along with the blog, Evelyn also started a grief support group on Facebook, under the same name, where members can share with one another in a supportive, non-judgmental environment.

In her spare time, Evelyn enjoys jigsaw puzzles, photography, and planning and creating items for special events. She also serves as First Lady and administrator of her church, On Good Ground Christian Fellowship, in Westampton, NJ. In addition to Joseph, she and her husband, Jeff, have two daughters, Brandi and Jasmine, and a grandson, Christian.

Photo Gallery

Joe at the mic.

Christmas family photo, from left: Jasmine, Jeff, Me,
Christian, Joseph, and Brandi.

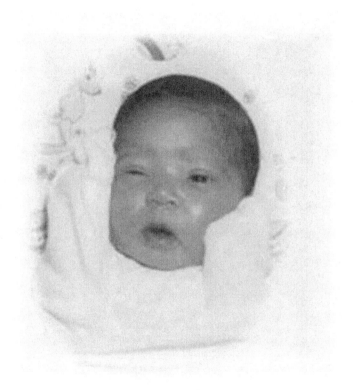

Joe as a newborn.

Joe at 3 months.

Even at age 2, Joe was writing.

This was Joseph's favorite position to watch TV. He used to lie across the bottom of the table, so we removed the glass from the top so he could sit in the squares and watch *Jurassic Park* over and over and over again.

Jeff and his little Joe.

Joe's favorite picture as a child (also the age he visited me). Joe often used it as his Facebook profile pic.

Jasmine and Joseph. She was always lovingly holding him captive in some way. (And he let her.)

Brandi and Joseph. Joseph was happy whenever he
was with his "Mama" Brandi.

Joseph in his "John Q" pose.

Joe and me one Sunday morning before church.

Brandi, Joseph, and Jasmine.

Joe giving me one of his great bear hugs. (My favorite picture.)

Joseph's graduation day picture. He was so happy.
(But not as happy as his mom and dad.)

Joe and Anthony. (This was their last pic taken together.)

Joe and Brandi one Christmas.

Joseph and Jasmine after church one Sunday.

Joe and me at Baltimore Oriole Stadium. As hot as it
was, he still wore his bowtie.

Jeff and Joe sharing a moment at Jeff's 50th birthday party. Joe shared how he was Jeff's biggest fan.

Joe and the Honda Civic he received for Christmas.

Joe and Jeff measuring curtains for Joe's space at Jeff's new office. (Joseph would start working with his dad.)

Joe and Christian (their last Christmas picture taken together.)

Group photo, from left: Christian, Jasmine, Brandi, and Joe.

The five of us after the funeral: Jasmine, Brandi, Christian, Jeff, and me. Everybody wore bowties and bright colors.

I love this picture of Joe from Christmas 2014. This was the last picture I got to take of him.

Joe's headstone (shaped like a bowtie) in Bordentown, New Jersey.

Made in the USA
Monee, IL
13 November 2019